LEADING YOUR CHILD
to
JESUS

Other books by David Staal

Leading Kids to Jesus: How to Have One-on-One Conversations about Faith

Making Your Children's Ministry the Best Hour of Every Kid's Week (With Sue Miller)

LEADING YOUR CHILD
to
JESUS

{ how parents can talk with their kids about faith }

DAVID STAAL

ZONDERVAN™

GRAND RAPIDS, MICHIGAN 49530 USA

WILLOW
Willow Creek Resources

ZONDERVAN.COM/
AUTHORTRACKER

Leading Your Child to Jesus
Copyright © 2006 by Willow Creek Association

Requests for information should be addressed to:
Zondervan, *Grand Rapids, Michigan 49530*

Library of Congress Cataloging-in-Publication Data

Staal, David.
  Leading your child to Jesus : how parents can talk with their kids about faith /
David Staal.
    p. cm.
  Includes bibliographical references (p.   ).
  ISBN-13: 978-0-310-26537-5
  ISBN-10: 0-310-26537-1
  1. Children—Conversion to Christianity. 2. Christian education of children.
I. Title.
  BV4925.S73 2006
  248.8'45—dc22

                                                                2005031944

Interior design by Beth Shagene

Illustrations by Liz Conrad

Printed in the United States of America

06 07 08 09 10 11 • 20 19 18 17 16 15 14 13 12 11 10 9 8 7 6 5 4 3 2

Contents

To Scott and Erin—
the relationship that each of you have with Jesus
served as my inspiration to write this book.

Foreword by Bill Hybels

Since the earliest days of pastoring Willow Creek Community Church, I've agonized over my sermons. Time and again, I've had to throw out first drafts and start over. Countless hours and multiple rewrites later, often even the messages I delivered left me feeling I could have done more to make this or that point a little clearer. But the second guessing I did on those communications paled by comparison to the weight that pressed down on me years ago as I pondered how to introduce Jesus to my two young children, Shauna and Todd. What was the best way to approach such critical discussions? I'll take the pressure of sermon preparation for 15,000 adults any day!

Thanks be to God, in his goodness and mercy, my children (now grown) love God, love his church, and understand grace. Apparently my fumbling attempts worked—and perhaps even more to the point, our army of Promiseland volunteers did yeoman's service for my kids (and thousands of others) by explaining and modeling God's persistent and pervasive love.

When it comes to daily conversations about God, parents everywhere feel that same responsibility to pass along the truth of our radically loving Savior to their kids. And now we don't need to feel alone or underequipped in that endeavor. David Staal has done all of us a great service by writing the book you hold in your hands. With wit and wisdom, his counsel will help us explain Scripture's life-giving message in language that children of all ages understand.

I'm hoping *Leading Your Child to Jesus* will serve a wide audience. Because when parents are equipped to talk with their children, families will be strengthened, churches will move forward, and God will be pleased. A new generation of Christ-followers is on deck, ready to make its mark on the world. But first, these children need their parents to provide them with clear and age-appropriate explanations of God's timeless truth and limitless love.

Read this book and you'll be better prepared to have those important discussions. And then watch God do what he alone can accomplish: remake a human heart.

BILL HYBELS
Senior Pastor
Willow Creek Community Church

Acknowledgments

Becky—Thanks for your love, encouragement, ideas, and all the time you gave me to write.

Erin and Scott—Thanks for your love, cheers, and all you contributed to this book.

Judy Keene—Thanks for your friendship and for your expertise to ensure every word worked as it should. And for rewriting those that didn't.

Teri Lange—Thanks for the research and the support you give me throughout every day. It's a blast doing ministry with you.

Pat Cimo—Thanks for all the hours you spent reviewing drafts, and for some great years of ministry together.

Sue Miller—Thanks for believing in me enough to choose me as a ministry partner, a friend, and as "e."

Bill Hybels—Thanks for building a church that offers opportunities for a guy like me to put my energy and talent to full use. (The jury's still out on the talent piece.)

Tammy Burke—Thanks for your support and constant reminders that I'm not crazy.

Paul Engle and Dawn Anderson—Thanks for your wisdom, edits, coaching, and confidence.

Starbucks team—The answer: 204 grandes or 25.5 gallons —roughly my entire body weight.

Promiseland programmers—Thanks for the creative assistance with wording.

Kristen Aikman—Thanks for your help crafting a conference session that has now grown up and become a book.

Garry Poole—Thanks for your deep friendship, ministry partnership, and for saying the words I needed to hear to start my walk with Christ.

Becky—Yes, you receive two acknowledgements because my love for you is greater than one acknowledgment could ever hold. I'm your man.

Prepare for a Moment's Notice

t's time; let's go."

Ninety seconds before I said those words, a nurse on the phone told me that my wife, Becky, was likely experiencing false labor. I'm no doctor, but I had a strong hunch her symptoms indicated the real thing. Intense pain squeezed my wife in intervals less than two minutes apart. My conclusion: we could wait no longer. "False" was wrong. It was time to act.

So we jumped in the car (I jumped, she waddled) and began a fifteen-mile journey to the hospital. As we pulled out of our subdivision, another contraction hit. Remembering our birthing class lessons, I offered, "Hee-hoo, hee-hoo," in an attempt to coach my wife's breathing. In an unusually deep and scary tone she responded, "Just drive fast." I stopped talking and started accelerating.

Two miles down the road we came upon the scene of an earlier accident that caused a long line of cars to form. However, desperate moments require daring measures. So I steered our car into the opposite lane and, with horn blasting and headlights flashing, approached the police officer who was directing traffic. We immediately caught his attention. He ran toward us, and I hoped he would arrest me so my wife could ride in a squad car to the hospital. While I started to explain our situation, the next contraction arrived and Becky let out a scream that caused the police dog in a nearby cruiser to whimper. "Get going!" the officer ordered, and our journey continued.

After racing at speeds I dare not put in print, we reached the hospital with little time to spare. Seven minutes later, our daughter Erin arrived in this world. I am so glad we chose to act and not wait—for the sake of my wife, my newborn daughter, and a dad totally unprepared for this delivery adventure.

There is another type of birth opportunity involving children that also requires parents to decide whether or not they will take action. Respected pollster George Barna conducted studies to determine the probability that people of various ages will ask Jesus to be their Savior—which, of course, designates spiritual birth. The results heavily favor children five through twelve years old (32 percent) compared to teens (4 percent) or adults age nineteen and older (6 percent). Barna's conclusion: "If people do not embrace Jesus Christ as their Savior before they reach their teenage years, their chance of doing so at all is slim."[1]

In other words, we must not wait to tell kids about Jesus. Instead, we need to take action.

To make the best use of the six chapters we'll spend together on this topic, let's start on the same page with this spiritual truth: kids *can* enter into a saving relationship with Jesus.

The Bible dispels any skepticism about the validity of a child's faith. Just look at Acts 2:39 in which Peter says, "The promise is for you and your *children* and for all who are far off—for all whom the Lord our God will call" (emphasis added). The Greek word used in this verse (*teknon*) literally means "child"—as in a daughter or son.[2] The promise Peter speaks of is salvation, and clearly it's available to kids. Romans 10:9 reveals the context of salvation: "If you confess with your mouth, 'Jesus is Lord,' and believe in your heart that God

raised him from the dead, you will be saved." This verse artic-
ulates the inclusive nature of God's saving grace and mandates
no minimum age.

Of course the ability to comprehend the promise, and the
timing in which it happens, varies by person—whether child
or adult. Focus on the Family's Dr. James Dobson describes
his salvation experience at age three.[3] Moody Bible Institute's
former president, Joe Stowell, accepted Christ at six.[4] Evan-
gelist Billy Graham made his decision at sixteen.[5] Although I
hesitate to mention my name in the same paragraph with the
previous three, I gave my life to Jesus at age twenty-nine (even
though still a kid at heart!).

So armed with assurance from Scripture that kids *can* enter
an authentic relationship with the Lord, along with numerous
examples that children *do* commit their young lives to Jesus,
the question becomes *how?* Good question—because *you*
might be the answer.

C. S. Lewis said, "There is nothing in the nature of the
younger generation which incapacitates them for receiving
Christianity. If any one is prepared to tell them, they are
apparently ready to hear."[6] You will serve your children well
when you are the one prepared to do that.

For clarity's sake, the focus of *Leading Your Child to Jesus* is
to equip parents like you and me to help our sons and daughters start a life of faith by accepting Jesus as Lord and Savior. Specifically, this preparation will center on building basic
skills for effective one-to-one conversations about key spiritual matters in language kids will understand. This topic fairly
bursts with importance because exciting and unpredictable
opportunities for these talks exist at home—even more often
than at church. The numbers aren't even close.

Reggie Joiner, Director of Family Ministries at North Point
Church in Atlanta, has done the math for us. "The average
church has about forty hours a year that they will have an

audience with a child," he says. "Parents have 3,000 hours in that same year. No one has more potential to influence a child's relationship with God than a parent."[7]

In addition to simple quantity of time, there is also a difference in the potential impact on a child. Reggie says, "The most awkward attempt of a father to pray with a son or daughter is a thousand times more powerful than the most seasoned believer who's not their parent, but might pray with that son or daughter."[8] That said, can you imagine the result if Mom and Dad could eliminate awkwardness by seeking advice on what to say and how to say it? Now you know the need this book seeks to meet.

Together we'll look at how and why to tell your story of becoming a Christian, the key components to share when you explain God's salvation plan, and an easily remembered prayer to start a relationship with Jesus. Along the way, we'll pick up communication tools and practices that will help with faith-focused conversations at any age—yours and that of your kids. Personal exercises follow each chapter to help you—possibly with your spouse or small group—get a firm, adept grip on these tools.

All of this preparation could lead to a profound payoff. It did for Beth, a ministry team colleague, while running an errand in the family car:

> One day while in the car, my four-year-old daughter asked what would happen if I died. I was caught a little off guard since we went from talking about the weather to talking about dying in the same brief exchange.
>
> Maty, very distressed, said, "Mom, I don't want you to die."
>
> I tried to comfort her. "Maty," I said, "you know I made a decision a long time ago to ask Jesus to be my forever friend. The Bible says if you love God and Jesus then you can go to heaven when you die. So you see, I'm not afraid of dying because I know that I'm going to heaven."

For the next couple of moments, I really felt like time had stopped. "Mom!" she said, with much excitement, "I love God and Jesus!"

"Well," I said, "have you ever asked him to forgive you and be your forever friend?"

She quietly said, "No."

I couldn't believe how God had prepared me to ask the next question. I had participated in some training at church a few times that readied me for exactly what to say next.

I continued to navigate through traffic, and with my hands gripped tightly on the steering wheel, I said, "Would you like to pray right now?"

She answered, "Yes." As we began to pray the salvation prayer, I was overwhelmed with gratitude. My own daughter was the first person I have ever had the privilege of praying the prayer with. I will be glad forever that I was prepared for that conversation—God used me!

Yes, Beth found herself in an ideal situation that doesn't often happen. However, she still had to respond to Maty with only a moment's notice—a condition we should expect. Beth knew the right words to say, but it's a safe bet that many of us would have succumbed to a variety of self-doubts regardless of the circumstances. What if I say something wrong? What if I'm asked a tough question? Do I know enough about the Bible? Can I put my faith into words? Finding the right words can be a challenge if they never receive forethought. But that can change.

As a parent, commit to becoming comfortable at speaking simple, personal faith explanations. Then you'll be ready for any car ride or bedtime conversation that offers a real-time salvation opportunity. Even if you feel fairly confident in your ability to have such discussions, commit to polishing your skills further. You'll celebrate your readiness when a child needs you.

My wife and I know firsthand that the concepts you're about to read actually work. We come nowhere near perfection as parents, but we have felt the thrill that comes from life-changing, heart-building conversations about Jesus with each of our children. We hope you experience the same. But that depends on you.

Each chapter in this book begins with a real-life experience at real amusement parks involving a real family—ours. And those stories will serve to illustrate points that can help prepare you for the moment when your words will help your son or daughter step closer to Jesus.

While you may relate to our amusement park adventures, reading about them will not be nearly as thrilling as experiencing them yourself. The same is true about the opportunity to lead your child to Jesus Christ. The real thrill happens when you experience it personally. And the journey to that end might very well begin the moment you commit to prepare —and then turn the page.

It's time; let's go.

CHAPTER 1

Communicating
with Kids

The forecast called for a hot, sticky day—and the weatherman's prediction was right on the mark. Although late July in the Midwest is a great time to swim in a pool, it is nowhere near the best time to trek through a crowded theme park. But there we were, my five-year-old son Scott and I, constantly seeking shade and drinking our weight in lemonade. Unfortunately, the fun was melting faster than the ice in our cups.

My spirits lifted when I spotted the Logger's Run. Simpler than most attractions, this ride featured a lazy float in a log-like boat along a river channel that led to a waterfall's brim. Then came a sudden long drop that bottomed out in a big wet splash, appearing to bring refreshment well worth a second or two of terror. "Hey Scott," I said, "want to go on this ride so we can cool off?"

"Sure," he replied.

Even the hour-plus wait in line took place in the shade, so it looked like smooth sailing to me. Finally our turn came to step into a log, and Scott and I took the front two spots of the log's four. I noticed no restraining bars, so concluded the drop must not be dangerous. Two teenage girls boarded the back seats, and our voyage began.

We meandered through the channel for a few minutes, then paused momentarily before we took the big plunge. Even though most logs skim the water surface at the bottom of the fall, ours didn't. Because Scott and I were in the first two seats, the log was very front heavy. Okay, to be fair, the weight imbalance was due to me. Regardless of the reason, the nose of our log dove into the water like a duck bobbing for food—and took all of us down with it. While most people get showered from the big splash, those aboard our log took a bath. We didn't sink in over our heads, but we definitely experienced 100 percent saturation from mid-torso down. And I loved it!

But I sat alone in my joy. The quiet ride to the disembark ramp hinted that a problem existed. The two girls and I quickly exited the log. Then, as I offered Scott a steady hand to step out, I asked him how he liked it. His response confirmed we had a problem. He burst into tears.

"What's wrong, buddy?" I asked.

"You didn't say we'd get wet!" he yelled back.

"Wait a minute," I reasoned, "what did you think I meant when I said we'd cool off?"

He paused to catch his breath and then blurted out, "I thought it was going to be air-conditioned!"

WHAT'S SAID VS. WHAT'S UNDERSTOOD

I'll never forget the lesson I learned as we stood there dripping in front of a crowd now staring at us: unless I'm careful, I can do a poor job of choosing words my children fully understand.

This is a common challenge for parents. Especially, it seems, for Christian moms and dads. Listen closely as some of them speak about spiritual life, and you may hear a language all its own. It might require years to learn—and that poses a problem. Christianity has the greatest message in the world, but it won't have any impact if it's delivered with descriptions that come close to being in code to those outside the circle.

This disconnect is even more obvious when it involves children. Sure, it may create humorous moments for parents to chuckle over or even write about in a book someday. But it also frequently, and unintentionally, stands in the way of meaningful dialogue about spiritual issues. Which is no laughing matter.

> Christianity has the greatest message in the world, but it won't have any impact if it's delivered with descriptions that come close to being in code to those outside the circle.

In *The Gentle Art of Communicating with Kids*, Dr. Suzette Elgin underscores this issue when she says, "The only meaning a sequence of language has is the meaning the listener understands it to have."[1] Consider the implications of her statement. It doesn't matter what you say; what matters is how a child *interprets* what you say. Basketball Hall of Fame coach Red Auerbach was on the same track when he offered a tip to coaches that lends itself to our topic: "It's not what you tell your players that counts; it's what they hear."[2]

This chapter was designed to help you close the gap between what you say and what your children understand you to have just said. Then the remainder of the book will build off the foundation laid by the following four key dynamics of communication with kids.

Dynamic 1 — Children understand concrete terms and language better than they understand abstract terms and language. In other words, children are likely to be much more literal than adults are with language. The parental application of this dynamic is easy: avoid symbolism or "religious" words. A few examples of what to steer clear of may help.

ᵉr phrase "perfect lamb who carried my sins" can
ₐd toward confusion. Why would a baby sheep
.... ᵣven relatively simple words can combine to form
complex phrases or analogies that encrypt the meaning from
children, who naturally assign literal meanings to words.

Jesus' disciples provide an excellent example of the confusion literal meaning can generate. In Matthew 16:6, Jesus
warns them, "Be on your guard against the yeast of the Pharisees and Sadducees." Even though the disciples heard him
speak in parables on other occasions, they jumped to a literal
translation of Jesus' imagery. They assumed he was referring
to their failure to pack bread for their journey. With a touch
of exasperation, he spelled out what he meant. "Then they
understood that he was not telling them to guard against the
yeast used in bread, but against the teaching of the Pharisees
and Sadducees" (verse 12).

Today's children should not be expected to understand
more than Christ's disciples! The answer to the dilemma of
abstract wording is to use concrete, or literal, terms. Clarity
requires that we use the words kids need to hear, even though
they're likely to differ from the words adults typically speak
to one another. There's nothing technically wrong with "laying
my sins at the foot of the cross," but the words "telling God I'm
sorry for the wrong things I've done" conveys the same message in a way a child can far more easily understand.

As your children grow older, their inability to process
abstract language will obviously decrease. But so does their
likelihood of becoming Christ-followers. As I mentioned earlier, pollster George Barna's research shows that children are
most likely to become Christians before age thirteen.[3] As a
person who beat the odds and gave my life to Christ as an
adult, I know that at any age, people outside the family of
God will benefit from concrete language in discussions about
faith. In 1 Corinthians 2:1, Paul gives us an excellent model

to follow: "When I came to you, brothers and sisters, I did not come proclaiming the mystery of God to you in lofty words or wisdom" (NRSV).

Dynamic 2 — Children are at different developmental levels. Age affects your child's ability to understand, no matter how simply you word the concepts you want to communicate. A child's age will combine with such factors as education, family and social surroundings, and life experiences to influence his or her intellectual and spiritual knowledge, and these factors will make a difference in how we communicate with our kids.

As a parent, I routinely see differences in my children's developmental levels. For example, my ten-year-old son works on long multiplication problems, while my seven-year-old daughter labors with double-digit addition. Neither is better than the other, they just occupy different learning levels based on their age difference. So in a one-to-one conversation, each child's respective age plays a role in determining the simplicity of the language and concepts I should use.

I recently learned — yet again — that age isn't the only factor. I coach my son's park district league basketball team. This season, a first-year player named Matthew joined our team of eight veterans. He's a great kid with a smile as big as the court we play on. During a scrimmage, I gave Matthew a specific assignment. "When the other team makes a basket," I said, "then you take the ball out of bounds."

"Okay, Coach," he replied with his signature grin.

Everyone on the team understood my instructions meant that after opponents scored, Matthew would grab the ball, step behind the black line under the basket, and then throw the ball to a teammate. Everyone, that is, except Matthew.

Moments later, a player on the other team sunk a basket, setting up Matthew's big role. Confidently, he grabbed the ball and stood behind the out-of-bounds line. And stood there. I whistled for play to stop, and asked Matt why he wasn't throwing the ball. The smile disappeared. I ran over to him, where he quietly informed me that I told him to take the ball out of bounds; I did not say to throw it to anyone.

He was right, and I was wrong. I did not consider Matthew's level of experience when I explained his assignment. I assumed that he would know what I meant. That moment prompted me to start coaching each player individually. We resumed practice with a wiser coach. Fortunately, Matthew's smile resumed as well.

The application to parents is clear—we must constantly self-check the assumptions that precede our comments. If your son has had little exposure to the Bible, then instead of referencing a story from Scripture, take a few moments to explain the story. Or when you encourage your daughter to pray, ensure

that she knows how to do that. Sensitivity to developmental levels swells in importance if you have more than one child. Likewise, this same issue deserves consideration before we take children into a church service designed for adults.

Sometimes a lack of knowledge, experience, or exposure is not the issue. Perhaps plenty of learning has taken place, which may or may not be a good thing. Some children have heard wonderful things about God and Jesus. Other kids recognize various names of God as the beginnings of curses from friends, family members, or television. This difference can become a big factor if the gospel is explained using an assumption of reverence for the Almighty.

Never hesitate to call a time-out to check whether your child understands what you're saying. Consider any assumptions you might be making. And always be willing to adapt your words to suit your listener. The more you tailor your comments to what you know about your child's developmental level, the better you will connect with him or her.

Dynamic 3—Children are most receptive to stories and terms they can relate to or picture. While growing up, I loved to watch the Peanuts television specials. As an adult, I still enjoy them. The story lines, characters, and timeless humor combine to serve as proof of Charles Schultz's genius. My favorite scenes among his numerous made-for-television shows were those times a kid sat in class listening to the teacher talk. The teacher, never shown, always said the same thing: "Wah, wah, wah, waaaah." Just the memory of that sound makes me chuckle as I write this paragraph.

Adults often quote the Peanuts teacher and her highly memorable lines. "Wah, wah, wah, waaaah" communicates jesting mockery of someone's longer-than-necessary droning on a subject, or delivery of a boring lecture. I remember, as a youngster, saying it once as I rolled my eyes in response to something my dad told me. Never tried it again.

The point is that no one, especially a child, enjoys a lecture. In fact, kids will understand far more of what an adult attempts to explain when that adult uses a brief story. Children love stories! Especially short ones. Kids will also engage with what's said at a deeper level when Mom or Dad uses words that refer to something familiar—creating a connection between the story and the listener. Let's look at a practical example.

I have a friend named Dennis who leads small groups of second- and third-grade boys in Promiseland, our church's children's ministry program. In this role, he inevitably has the opportunity to speak with them about his journey to Jesus. When he shares his story, he starts by saying, "Guys, I'd like to tell you a story about a young guy your age who liked to play baseball, soccer, and basketball. He wasn't always the best kid on the team, and didn't always get picked first to play." For the next minute or two, saucer-sized eyes follow Dennis and his every word.

One reason Dennis is so effective at sharing his testimony is his ability to draw kids in — they want to hear what he has to say. He tells them a story, rather than lecturing. He seasons that story with points that are familiar to second- and third-grade boys. If a boy likes sports, he'll relate to Dennis' tale. If he doesn't like sports, he'll relate to how the boy in the story didn't get picked first to play.

Jesus was the master at story-based teaching. He told the tale of the good Samaritan (Luke 10) in response to a question that he could easily have answered with a fact or lecture on who to consider as a neighbor. Instead, he illustrated — through a story — the concept of "neighbor" in a way no one would ever forget.

We too can use this technique, which is sometimes referred to as painting a word picture. If I include one or more parallels to my son or daughter's life in what I say, he or she can picture the scenario and engage in the conversation. Finding a commonality to mention is easy for parents — we do it already without much thought. Sometimes you can rewind the memory of your own life and describe a personal experience. Think of all the times you've said, "When I was a kid ..." For even greater impact, though, relate directly to your child's *current* life. For instance, "You know how you have lots of choices about what to play during recess ..." or some similar statement lets kids know that what follows will directly apply to them — an approach that will capture attention far more easily than a lecture.

Another way to engage a child in a story is through well-timed questions that spark thoughts but don't require extended pondering. Have you ever observed someone do this particularly well? That question invites your brief mental participation as a reader, but doesn't go down a long tangent. Examples of such questions in conversation include: "Have you ever thought about that?" "Can you imagine how she felt?" "You've never done that, have you?" (followed by a quick smile). The list could go on for pages.

These questions don't require long responses, if any at all. We use them, instead, to provoke thought. They involve the listener. They allow you to talk *with* your child rather than *at* him. And they keep you from sounding like the Peanuts teacher.

Dynamic 4—Children may focus on, or be distracted by, a single detail in a story. This dynamic serves as a qualifier to the stories we will tell. Like many people, my life's been full of ups and downs, bumps and bruises, and plenty of valuable lessons. A generous amount of that learning occurred while I worked in the National Football League. But if I start to tell another person about any life issue I tackled during my brief stint with the Indianapolis Colts, the conversation typically takes an abrupt turn. The person I'm talking with attempts to picture me in full pads and a helmet and usually ventures a guess at what position I played. The disappointment lasts only a moment when I reveal that I worked in the public relations department!

Now imagine if I were to mention this life experience while sharing my personal testimony with my fifth-grade son. He might insist I tell him about an interview I conducted with Bears running back Walter Payton, and then I'd have to struggle to bring the conversation back to the original spiritual topic. So I've learned to carefully consider the details in any story I tell my kids.

Consider the impact of telling your son or daughter about how Jesus helped you conquer alcohol or drug abuse. Of course Christ can prove victorious in such a situation; that's not the issue. Nor is the issue concealing an unattractive truth from your kids. The issue is one of appropriateness and timing. Choose the right time to reveal details in your personal story—using the earlier dynamic about developmental levels as your guide. I heard a parent say to a young girl, "One day you and your brother will understand how great it is to have each other as friends." Obviously upset with her brother, the girl replied, "I know. But that day isn't today."

Susan Shadid, Promiseland's training director, offers a valuable perspective on considering details as they relate to a much more common conversation topic. She specifically advises

Reexamine our details
and be sensitive
to their impact
on our listeners.

adults not to dwell too heavily on heaven as the sole reason for salvation. "Spending eternity with God in heaven is a cornerstone of becoming a Christian that kids need to understand," she says. "But if that's the exclusive focus, some kids—especially younger ones—could become scared of Christianity because they might believe people who accept Christ have to die soon after."

Don't misinterpret this dynamic. It doesn't advise us to refrain from storytelling or to leave out key spiritual truths. The counsel is to reexamine our details and to be sensitive to their impact on our listeners. Often, we simply need to reword what we say in a way that maintains meaning without introducing distractions.

STARTING POINTS

If you feel it is a significant challenge to apply the four communication dynamics every time you chat with your kids, then you are exactly right. Success will come with practice—and that's okay. I've taught these dynamics for several years, but still have to throw the penalty flag on myself every now and then. A realistic and wise starting point is to actively listen to the descriptive language kids use when you're around. While driving to dance lessons or when kids play in your yard, pay attention to conversations your children have with others.

A valuable exercise to try before you have the opportunity for a faith discussion with your child is to take a few moments to imagine what life is like for your son or daughter. Picture in your mind right now what you might say about the basics of Christianity. What do you think would make sense to her? What commonalities exist between your child's life and yours when you were growing up? What connections exist between the unique life he experiences and truths in the Bible? (Hint—the list is quite long.) The challenge here is to give thought to what you might say, applying the four dynamics, *before* you have to say it.

For more specific preparation, discover how other kids— similar in age to your own children—describe their relationships with Jesus, and tune in closely to their words. Your church's children's ministry might be the place to turn for this assistance, or possibly another family. In case you're not in a position to make this request easily and naturally, I will lend you my daughter's assistance. When she was seven years old, she wrote her thoughts about being in a relationship with Jesus as if she were telling a friend. I call it the Gospel According to Erin. Here's what she wrote (with plenty of help from our computer's auto spelling/grammar function):

> You have to know Jesus before you do it [pray]. You have to know that he came down to earth for us. He explained to people how to live and treat people nice. So that we could go to heaven, he died on a cross. It's like people know him here, but he's really in heaven, but not dead. Jesus cleans us of the wrong things we've done just like taking a bath with soap.
>
> This is how to be a forever friend with Jesus! Just pray—"In my life, I have done a lot of stuff wrong and I want to go to heaven. So I want what Jesus did when he died to count for me. Please be with me all my life, and help me live my life like you want me to. Amen!"
>
> But you can only be somebody's best friend if you meet them, and that's how you need to be with Jesus—you need to meet him and get to know him and then say that prayer.
>
> The coolest part of being Jesus' forever friend is that he is always with you! Sometimes I say, "Jesus, I'm scared, help me." Then sometimes he makes me not scared. But when he doesn't, I just run into Mom and Dad's room.
>
> I wish everyone could be Jesus' friend.

Erin uses simpler words than you and I might normally select. Yet her language still communicates the message of Christ, and would likely prove effective with young listeners.

Adopting a manner that focuses on the listener is a worthy challenge, but not a new concept. In Acts 2, on the day of Pentecost when the Holy Spirit descended upon the believers, the wind howled and what looked like tongues of fire touched all who were there. What happened next relates to our challenge. The people outside of the building in which all of this happened heard individuals speaking in their native languages —and the multicultured words seemed to come from the homogenous group of Christ-followers. The reaction was one of astonishment; "We hear them declaring the wonders of God in our own tongues!... What does this mean?" (verses 11–12).

For us, it means that when we keep in mind the four key dynamics of communicating with kids, then we will declare the wonders of God in ways that they will understand—no tongues of fire required! These principles will increase the effectiveness of conversations with children regardless of the topic. Besides, kids think it's cool when an adult explains something to them in a way that they truly understand.

So let's put the four key dynamics to work. The next chapter walks through step-by-step training to prepare any adult to share his or her own story about becoming a Christian. After that, we'll look at explaining the plan of salvation, then how to help a child pray to become a Christ-follower.

Personal Exercises

1. Write down several examples of abstract terms and language you've heard used in church or from other adults that likely confuse kids. Have you ever used any of them yourself?

2. Describe what you believe each of your children already understands about God, Jesus, and the Bible.

3. Develop a list of bullet points that describes your kids' lives today. In addition to school, culture, and fun activities, include typical attitudes toward God, Jesus, church, and Christianity. Underline items similar to your own childhood years.

CHAPTER 2

Share Your Story

The honor of being the best-known theme park belongs to Disney World in Orlando, Florida. A visit to Disney thrills virtually any child. In fact, merely the anticipation of the trip generates fun. At least it did for my wife and me, which prompted us to announce to our kids, "We're going to Disney World!" a full year prior to our trip. We intended to squeeze as much excitement as possible out of the entire experience—and that included the planning process.

So while I spent months whooping up excitement at home, my wife practically earned an advanced degree in Disney trip planning. Phone calls, conversations with other families, books, Web searches—she did it all. And when we arrived, we followed her detailed plan to make the most of every moment. My job was to carry the luggage. With a smile.

The result of Becky's tireless research was a trip that overachieved its potential for joy because we knew the hot spots, cool rides, and strategies to avoid long lines. Although several books claim to give you great tips about Disney, we found that the stories and recommendations from people we know always proved to be golden advice.

This was especially true for our daughter, Erin. Her best friend, Lauren, repeatedly told her that the coolest ride at Disney is Space Mountain—an enormous indoor roller coaster that shoots you through space. Unfortunately for me, in addition to luggage duty I'm also the designated rider. Based on Lauren's enthusiastic endorsement of Space Mountain, Erin's mind was made up that we would spend every spare moment tossed to the outer reaches of the galaxy. I prefer roller coasters located in daylight, where I can see what drop or turn approaches (when my eyes are open, that is). But I did my job. With a smile.

To be fair, other Disney attractions also offer worthy challenges to someone like me. In hindsight, I'm not sure which experience gripped me most intensely—the feeling that my life would end on Space Mountain or wishing it would end on the boat ride that featured thousands of dolls chanting, "It's a small world after all." Fortunately, the latter did not make Lauren's recommendation list, so it had no chance of making the "let's go on it again" roster we kept. But Space Mountain did.

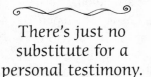

There's just no substitute for a personal testimony.

After our third turn battling death-by-roller coaster in near darkness, I understood the high value kids place on other people's experiences. Without her friend's personal testament and encouragement, my daughter and I would have braved other adventures. But we trusted her buddy because friends can be counted on to tell the truth—much more so than any messages, signs, or persuasion offered by other attractions. There's just no substitute for a personal testimony.

As much fun as Space Mountain is (if you're Erin or Lauren), the thrill pales in comparison to the most incredible ride in life—a relationship with Jesus. Just ask any Christ-follower to share his or her personal testimony. Or should you? Just because a person has a story doesn't guarantee his or her ability to share it well. Fortunately, a reasonable dose of preparation is all that's needed to sharply increase the odds that it will be effective.

THE BASICS OF A STRONG TESTIMONY

The very best way to begin that preparation is to consider the story of how you became a Christian. Why that story? Because a personal testimony carries considerable weight. It offers real value to your son or daughter because from the moment of birth, his or her eyes have looked up to you. When you share your journey to faith, you illustrate that Jesus changes real people's lives today, not just the lives of folks in the Bible two thousand years ago. In today's world, children receive messages about religion and Christianity from many sources—some good and some not. A testimony makes the vast concepts of Christianity intensely personal and believable, because the source of information is Mom or Dad. And that's good.

Consider this analogy: a conversation about football with buddies around the watercooler is very different from a conversation about football with an NFL player. Why? Because with the player, you can discuss actual game experience with someone who plays the sport, not one who simply watches and talks about it. Likewise, you begin from a unique position of already holding your child's trust—meaning parents start with home-field advantage when tackling a topic like personal faith.

Willow Creek's senior pastor Bill Hybels affirms the value of such a conversation: "The greatest gift you can give someone is the story of Jesus and how he changes lives—especially yours."[1]

This gift needs thoughtful wrapping, though, to make it effective. To that end, Bill lists key attributes worthy of careful attention:[2]

> Make it clear.
> Use the right terminology.
> Keep it short.

Left unattended, my story would run counter to these guidelines. Maybe yours would too. Add to this list a requirement to relate well to kids, and the need for work becomes obvious. The rest of this chapter will help us craft and polish our personal stories, enabling us to confidently and effectively share them with our children.

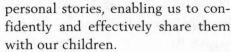

Think of your testimony as what follows the lead-in statement, "Here's what happened to me."

Think of your testimony as what follows the lead-in statement, "Here's what happened to me." Then recognize your responsibility to communicate that story well. A worthwhile challenge indeed, when you consider the potential outcome: You can help your son or daughter understand *his or her* need for a personal relationship with Jesus when you share the story of *your* personal relationship with Jesus. In other words, God will become important to them if they know that God is important to you. And according to 1 Peter 2:9, that's a duty we each own:

> But you are the ones chosen by God, chosen for the high calling of priestly work, chosen to be a holy people, God's instruments to do his work and speak out for him, to tell others of the night-and-day difference he made for you. (MSG)

So let's work on our stories.

COACHING FROM AN APOSTLE

We'll base our testimonies on a three-part outline designed to serve as a memory tool and an organizational aid. To deliver your story, you must be able to quickly remember it. And to deliver your story well requires that you articulate it with logic that another person can easily follow. Mark Mittelberg, Bill Hybels, and Lee Strobel, authors of the *Becoming a Contagious Christian* training course, suggest that we follow the direction found in Acts 26 and examine the three-part approach used by Paul.

His testimony contains three very distinct, sequential periods of time. While we look at Paul's words, consider your own story and life experiences, and specifically how you would describe your life using these three eras: before becoming a Christian (call it "BC"), your conversion ("the Cross"), and life after becoming a Christian ("AD"). Questions along the way will prompt you through this self-reflection process; your answers will serve as building blocks later in the chapter.

BC (before becoming a Christian)

Paul begins his personal testimony to King Agrippa with a description of life before becoming a Christ-follower:

> The Jews all know the way I have lived ever since I was a child, from the beginning of my life in my own country, and also in Jerusalem. They have known me for a long time and can testify, if they are willing, that according to the strictest sect of our religion, I lived as a Pharisee. And now it is because of my hope in what God has promised our fathers that I am on trial today. This is the promise our twelve tribes are hoping to see fulfilled as they earnestly serve God day and night. O king, it is because of this hope that the Jews are accusing me. Why should any of you consider it incredible that God raises the dead?
>
> I too was convinced that I ought to do all that was possible to oppose the name of Jesus of Nazareth. And that is just what I did in Jerusalem. On the authority of the chief priests I put many of the saints in prison, and when they were put to death, I cast my vote against them. Many a time I went from one synagogue to another to have them punished, and I tried to force them to blaspheme. In my obsession against them, I even went to foreign cities to persecute them.
>
> Acts 26:4–11

Paul uses very specific language that paints a vivid picture of him as a zealous Pharisee and staunch oppressor of Jesus' followers. The importance of such descriptors is that they set up the life change that Jesus brings, and they'll also work well for Christians today. Everyone had life experience before they met Jesus as Lord and Savior. Most are not as vicious as Paul's, yet all of us were equally lost. Because this era is before Christ, it's referred to as BC.

To help stimulate ideas for the BC era, write key words that come to mind when considering these two questions:

1. What were you like, personally and/or spiritually, before becoming a Christ-follower?

2. What caused you to begin considering a move toward God/Christ?

The Cross (conversion)

In Acts 26:12 – 18, Paul provides details of his conversion along the Damascus road:

> On one of these journeys I was going to Damascus with the authority and commission of the chief priests. About noon, O king, as I was on the road, I saw a light from heaven, brighter than the sun, blazing around me and my companions. We all fell to the ground, and I heard a voice saying to

me in Aramaic, "Saul, Saul, why do you persecute me? It is hard for you to kick against the goads."

Then I asked, "Who are you, Lord?"

"I am Jesus, whom you are persecuting," the Lord replied. "Now get up and stand on your feet. I have appeared to you to appoint you as a servant and as a witness of what you have seen of me and what I will show you. I will rescue you from your own people and from the Gentiles. I am sending you to them to open their eyes and turn them from darkness to light, and from the power of Satan to God, so that they may receive forgiveness of sins and a place among those who are sanctified by faith in me."

In these verses, Paul clearly recounts how he met Jesus, and he does so in a manner easy to understand. Notice that the description remains tightly focused on Paul's experience and does not expand into a lecture on the salvation plan. Because this era is the point Christ enters Paul's life and converts him, it's called "the Cross."

To help stimulate ideas for the Cross era, write key words that come to mind when considering these two questions:

1. What realization did you come to that finally motivated you to follow Christ?

2. Specifically, what did you do to become a Christian?

AD (after becoming a Christian)

The third part of the story in Acts 26 features Paul's life after his conversion:

> So then, King Agrippa, I was not disobedient to the vision from heaven. First to those in Damascus, then to those in Jerusalem and in all Judea, and to the Gentiles also, I preached that they should repent and turn to God and prove their repentance by their deeds. That is why the Jews seized me in the temple courts and tried to kill me. But I have had God's help to this very day, and so I stand here and testify to small and great alike.
>
> verses 19–22

Deep contrast exists between the Paul in Acts 26:19–22 and the man described in 4–11. And therein lies the power of a personal testimony—a life clearly changed as a result of Jesus. Because Paul describes the different man he became after Jesus entered the picture, this era is known as AD.

To help stimulate ideas for the AD era, write key words that come to mind when considering these two questions:

1. How did your life begin to change after you began to follow Christ?

2. What are clear differences in your life now that you follow Christ, compared with your BC life?

MODERN-DAY TESTIMONIES

The BC-Cross-AD formula worked well for Paul and continues to serve the same purpose today. Let's look at two modern-day testimonies as proof.

Dennis Tells His Story

In the previous chapter I mentioned my friend Dennis. He leads a small group of third-grade boys every Sunday, and has become quite proficient at sharing his story with kids either one-to-one or in clusters. After years of experience, Dennis skillfully weaves together a three-part outline with the four communication dynamics covered in chapter 1 to deliver a testimony children love to hear. We can learn plenty from this seasoned veteran as we prepare to develop our own stories.

BC

"I know a story about a young guy who was about eight years old. He loved to play baseball, soccer, and especially basketball. Now he wasn't the best kid on the team all the time and he didn't always get picked first, but when he played, he played really hard. He also went to church almost every week and learned lots of stories in the Bible.

"One day there was a story about how Jesus had to die on the cross and he didn't even deserve to. So after church this young guy told his mom about the story. She asked if he would like to talk to the pastor to hear more about the story. The little guy said okay.

"He was kind of nervous, but he still went and sat down to talk with the pastor. He found out the pastor was really a pretty good guy, and that it was pretty comfortable to talk with him. The pastor asked if he had ever done anything that his mom and dad had not wanted him to do. Well, he couldn't really lie to the pastor, so he said yes. The pastor said that those things are what God calls sins. And that's why Jesus had to do what he did—it was to get rid of all our sins. The pastor asked him if he would like to pray about his sin now. And the boy said okay, but he was really nervous. The pastor started praying, but noticed that this little boy wasn't praying with him. So the pastor asked God to help the boy come to know him more."

The Cross

"Well, that guy continued going to church for a long time, and he continued to play basketball and did stuff like the rest of the guys. As a matter of fact, one day he ended up being the captain of his basketball team. His small group leader was there for one game, and after it was over, he explained to a group of boys that in the Bible it says we need to go and talk to Jesus and ask him to be our friend. And nobody can do that for us. Immediately, the boy thought back to the time when he was sitting with the pastor, and how the pastor prayed he would become a good friend of God. He realized he had never really told Jesus himself that he needed to be forgiven for all he had done wrong. So right then, he prayed with his small group leader for Jesus to be his friend, for Jesus to forgive him, and for Jesus to make sure he could go to heaven one day."

AD

"From that point on, this guy knew that Jesus would always be with him, and that he was going to spend forever in heaven.

"The reason I tell you guys this story is that I know it's true. I know it's true because this is my story. You see, after talking with my small group leader I understood that all I had to do was pray to start a real friendship with Jesus. And that's what I did. If you are ready to pray to Jesus, I'd love to do that with you just like my small group leader did with me. But if you're not ready yet, that's okay too. We can spend as much time as you want talking about this to help you really figure it out for yourself."

My Testimony

I've had several opportunities to share my own story: while talking with my own children, during our children's ministry's salvation weekends, and in conversations with other adults. The three paragraphs that follow contain the words I'm likely to say after "Here's what happened to me."

BC

"I grew up going to church every weekend where I heard a lot about the Bible. Have you ever had to learn a lot about something, but you really didn't understand what it meant? I admit that I really didn't see the need to care about what happened to people so long ago. And because of that attitude, God seemed to be a long way from my world. That belief, unfortunately, allowed me to do a lot of stuff that I knew wasn't right. Who cared about a God who was way, way out there when I wasn't getting caught doing wrong stuff right here? For many years—until I was twenty-nine—my life was a lot of fun high points followed by difficult low times."

The Cross

"Then Uncle Jim and Aunt Sarah invited Mom and me to a church. At first we went so that we'd have a place to go at Christmas and Easter because we didn't have a church of our own to attend. But we liked that church and decided to keep going each week. Then one Sunday, I heard a message about God wanting to have a personal relationship with individual people—even people like me. For the first time in my life, I understood what a relationship with God meant and it sounded good to me. I heard that I could start this friendship by just praying to Jesus, so I did."

AD

"And now, guess what? I still have good times and not so good times, but that's okay because Jesus is with me no matter what, just like a best friend. I love living every day amazed and grateful that he is close to someone like me—guiding me, helping me, and loving me."

TELLING YOUR OWN STORY

We should highlight two key points about testimonies. First, both stories you just read definitely qualify as child-appropriate, but would likely change if used with grown-ups. When I share my testimony with other adults, I typically add details in the BC and AD eras that bring clarity to my highs and lows. But because I filter my comments through the four communication dynamics, especially regarding details that might distract, I employ a different approach with kids. The essence of my story, though, remains unchanged.

Second, people who experience salvation at a very young age might wonder if the BC-Cross-AD approach will work for them. If you fall into this category, though, I believe you have an advantage over those of us saved later in life. The fact that at a young age you made the decision to become a Christian establishes strong common ground with your children. So unapologetically include statements that begin with "When I was about your age ...," "Something cool happened to me when I was six ...," or other words that allow you to go back and be a kid again—and will capture the attention of your son or daughter.

People who experience salvation at a very young age might wonder if the BC-Cross-AD approach will work for them.

Whether your story is from your childhood or a more recent period, the length will pose a challenge. If you were to write your testimony this moment, there's a strong likelihood that you would join Dennis and me with a version as long as Acts 26. Chances are also good that you'd never remember it. So don't start writing yet. We're going to simplify.

Fortunately, the apostle Paul helps us once again. In Galatians 1:13–17, he shares a much shorter conversion story:

> For you have heard of my previous way of life in Judaism, how intensely I persecuted the church of God and tried to destroy it. I was advancing in Judaism beyond many Jews of my own age and was extremely zealous for the traditions of my fathers. But when God, who set me apart from birth

So after you finish reading this chapter, write four sentences that capture your story of becoming a Christian.

Start with each era's key words that you jotted down earlier. Then add details as needed. For now, though, focus on fashioning four sentences that will easily come to mind when needed. Once done, you can share your testimony any time. And with the reality of attention spans, four sentences might be all you get. So give it all you've got while you write. Additional four-sentence examples appear at the end of this chapter.

Filter

Don't forget to apply the four communication dynamics from the previous chapter to keep the language of your story

kid-friendly. To filter your story with the dynamics, refer to these questions while you write:

BC
1. Is this a condition or lifestyle to which my child can relate? If no, then simplify.
2. Will my child be distracted by my sinful past or lifestyle details? If yes, then reword or delete.

The Cross
1. Is it clear that I took some action when I accepted Christ? If no, think more specifically.
2. Is what I did understandable and applicable to a child? If no, then reword.

AD
1. Is the change Christ made in my life easy to understand? If no, then describe the change differently, or focus on a different type of change.
2. Do I make description of my life as a Christian clear to my child? If no, then simplify by using words kids might say when they describe aspects of life.

Refine

To strengthen your story further, consider Paul's shortest testimony in Galatians 1:23. Using limited words, he acknowledges that he used to persecute the church and now proclaims its faith. Or look in John 9 at the man who says he was once blind and now he sees. Both of these one-sentence descriptions show the marked difference between BC life and AD life. "Persecute" becomes "proclaim." "Blind" becomes "I see." Why? Jesus made the difference. Structure your story so that it too shows identifiable life change.

Organizing your story and refining it into four easy-to-remember sentences requires effort, so expect the process to

Personal Exercises

1. Write your story:

   My Story

   1. _____

   _____

   _____

   _____

   2. _____

   _____

   _____

   _____

   _____

   3. _____

   _____

   _____

   _____

   4. _____

   _____

   _____

   _____

2. Read your four sentences aloud and time yourself. If it's longer than one minute, cut down your sentence length.

3. Share your four sentences with at least two other adults. Ask for feedback on clarity. Make changes as needed.

Additional Examples of Four-Sentence Testimonies:

Peggy
Madison, WI

1. Before I became a Christian, I went to Sunday school and played nicely with my sister and my friends and I was a good girl.

2. But I learned from the Bible that I couldn't go to heaven just because I was a good kid!

3. So I asked Jesus to forgive the wrong things that I had done and to be my friend forever.

4. And now I know that one day, I will be in heaven with Jesus forever, that Jesus will always be with me and help me every day, and I can learn more about him by reading the Bible and praying to him.

Angie
Grandville, MI

1. I grew up going to church and Sunday school but I didn't live the way Jesus wanted me to live.

2. When I was in fifth grade something scary and lonely happened to me.

3. I then realized that the only way I could make it through this scary and lonely time would be to accept Jesus.

4. Since then I don't feel lonely or scared because I know Jesus is my friend.

"This must be the world's largest ice cream cone," I said. "Do you think we can eat it all?" Filled with a purpose, we ate for the next thirty minutes. Actually, I made sure Scott did most of the eating. And after a heroic effort that required more than twenty napkins, we declared the cone as winner because it still held about two dollars' worth of vanilla-chocolate swirl. Maybe cowinner is a better word—I shared the victory because Scott couldn't eat another thing for more than two hours.

The reason for this story is not to illustrate the potential downfalls caused by parents who allow kids to make nutritional decisions. Nor is it a lesson on cash management. The point is this—Scott heard a great plan and opted to take advantage of it. To do so, he had to understand the plan I explained to him, and he had to see how it personally applied to him.

Hearing the Greatest Plan in Mexico

In a similar fashion, our kids need to hear us tell them about the greatest plan—the gospel plan of salvation through Jesus Christ. And although the plan makes perfect sense to Christian adults, explaining it in ways that sons and daughters will personally understand can present a big challenge. Without forethought and preparation, a salvation explanation can easily sound like we're speaking in a foreign tongue.

> Although the plan makes perfect sense to Christian adults, explaining it in ways that sons and daughters will personally understand can present a big challenge.

A few years ago my wife and I served on a mission trip to an orphanage in Baja California, Mexico. Each day we joined child evangelism teams that visited camps filled with kids left to fend for themselves as older siblings and parents worked in area tomato fields. These beautiful kids loved seeing the orphanage vans filled with adults; they knew that the sole reason for our trip was to visit with them.

Regrettably, my Spanish fluency consisted of questions about age and the location of the nearest bathroom. Because of this language deficiency, my task list included the following: (1) drive the van, (2) carry supplies, (3) set up a small area for the Bible study, and (4) let kids climb on me. Oh yes, and smile. After just a few short minutes, I knew everyone's age and the locations of several bathrooms. Then the real teachers took over.

"Jesus is willing to always be with you" is a comforting message to kids left alone each day until they're old enough for field work. But considering the audience, I would never have dreamed of trying to convey Jesus' message in English. These bright-eyed kids needed to hear it in words they could personally understand. In similar fashion, we parents face a challenge to explain the greatest message in the world using terms that make sense to our children.

KID-TALK BASICS

Fortunately, sharing the salvation plan with children does not require you to learn a second language. In fact, just as you worked with your testimony in the previous chapter, we'll work on developing basic kid-talk that involves simple and familiar terms. To do this requires two considerations: First, know the story to tell. Second, use the right words.

Know the Story to Tell

One morning at breakfast, a discussion between Shari and her six-year-old son, Nicky, began with his choice of cereals and then moved to a description of his fascinating dream the night before. As often happens with kids, the topic took another quick turn into his thoughts about Jesus. Shari later related: "It led to a great conversation about Christ and that after we receive his gift, we never have to doubt our relationship with him."

Way to go, Shari—she made the most of that moment! But if you were in her slippers that morning, do you have confidence that you would've known what to say and how to say it during breakfast with young Nicky?

Check your local bookstore or search the Internet and you'll find entire books, videos, and websites that communicate what it means to be a Christian. But while you can share these books or other materials with an adult, interacting with a child requires different preparation—especially when you consider his or her typically short attention span. The brief window of opportunity to address a kid's interest opens and shuts quicker than snap, crackle, pop. To that end, your challenge is to know the basic tenets of faith so you can clearly share them in a minute or two. Sometimes you'll have more time. Sometimes you'll have less. But regardless of the time available, knowing the basics is the place to start.

The *Becoming a Contagious Christian* evangelism training course suggests remembering the gospel using a four-part outline:

1. God
2. Us
3. Christ
4. You and me

Equipped with the four components of God's story, you can share them whenever and however the need arises. Popular gospel illustrations such as the Bridge, the Wordless Book, and other tools are—at their core—clever deliveries of this same message. Craig Jutila, children's pastor at Saddleback Church, in Lake Forest, California, has it right when he says, "The message doesn't change; just the method."[1]

Before we examine method, though, let's fully understand the message—segment by segment:

1. God

- He is a holy God, perfect in every way. Nothing else in this world fits the description of being perfect, so everything will fall short in a comparison to God. Yet, he created people to be like himself, along with an expectation of holiness or perfection.

  Be holy because I, the Lord your God, am holy.
  Leviticus 19:2

- He is a loving God, who loves each of us more than we can imagine. In fact, God created love.

  We love because he first loved us.
  1 John 4:19

- He is a just God, so he doesn't turn the other way and ignore sin.

  For I the Lord love justice; I hate robbery and wrongdoing.
  Isaiah 61:8 (NRSV)

2. Us

- All people commit sin. And when compared to God's beautiful standard of perfection, sin paints an ugly picture of a person.

  For all have sinned and fall short of the glory of God.
  Romans 3:23

Use the Right Words

The explanation for the gospel that we just went through, while perfectly understandable to an adult, would earn a very low kid-friendly rating based on my word choices. Abstract phrases abound, as does language that will fly past kids at the speed of sound.

Rewording the gospel—is that legal? Yes. Our language provides us with word options that do an excellent job of preserving its meaning. The entire reason to explain the gospel is in hopes that your son or daughter will make a life-changing decision based on personally understanding and believing God's plan. Without kid-friendly words, any salvation explanation collapses—even the time-honored Bridge will seem to be an odd stick-figure drawing and the Wordless Book will fall on innocently deaf ears. Complex vocabulary comprehension should not exist as a prerequisite to the free gift of grace.

> Rewording the gospel—is that legal? Yes. Our language provides us with word options that do an excellent job of preserving its meaning.

Acts 14:1 states the need for—and benefit of—sharing the salvation plan in listener-focused language: At Iconium Paul and Barnabas went as usual into the Jewish synagogue. There they spoke so effectively that a great number of Jews and Gentiles believed. The original Greek words translate into "spoke in a manner." Paul didn't alter the meaning or message of the gospel; he simply modified his verbal delivery to accommodate his listeners. The words "great number of Jews and Gentiles" indicate that this approach yielded significant success.

In 1 Corinthians, Paul reveals that this manner-modifying approach became a deliberate strategy that stretched past Iconium:

To the Jews I became like a Jew, to win the Jews. To those under the law I became like one under the law (though I myself am not under the law), so as to win those under the law. To those not having the law I became like one not having the law (though I am not free from God's law but am under Christ's law), so as to win those not having the law. To the weak I became weak, to win the weak. I have become all things to all men so that by all possible means I might save some. I do all this for the sake of the gospel, that I may share in its blessings.

1 Corinthians 9:20–23

The gospel Paul shared in the first century with residents of what is now Konya, Turkey, is the same gospel message to share with our children in the twenty-first century. And just as they did in Paul's day, the words we use deserve attention.

Kid-Talk Fluency

To start, we'll pull out key words from the four-part gospel description above. Then we'll find child-appropriate words that preserve the biblical message. To make this easy, the chart that follows provides kid-friendly terms that bring strong, yet simple meaning to a handful of terms used frequently by adults. However, the right-hand column is not in the same order as the left, so take a moment and draw lines between the synonymous phrases. An answer key follows.

Common terms

1. Sin
2. Punishment
3. Crucify
4. Savior
5. Resurrection
6. Ask Jesus into your heart
7. Leadership (be Lord)

Kid-friendly terms

A. Someone who agrees to be in trouble for us
B. Died on a cross because in so much trouble
C. Follow what Jesus says, ask him for help to do the right thing
D. Ask him to forgive you and always be your friend
E. Not nice, wrong things we do
F. Get in trouble, time-out, spanking
G. Didn't stay dead

(1-E, 2-F, 3-B, 4-A, 5-G, 6-D, 7-C)

Notice that the kid-friendly phrases share the same meaning as the common terms; they just use commonsense word choices that focus on young listeners. You have to admit, that if you tell your son the blood of the lamb will wash away sins, he will think you are pretty gross. But if you tell your daughter that Jesus offers to be in trouble for all the wrong stuff we do, you stand a good chance at capturing her attention. While the manner can be modified, the meaning stays the same. And maybe a life changes as a result.

Common sense dictates that different ages will require different words. The key to success is your willingness to throw religious-sounding words out the window and modify your terminology. So brainstorm for a few minutes. Ask God to help you bring new words to mind. You need only a few to make the story, his story, clear to your son or daughter. What are the ages of your children? What cultural considerations should influence your word choice? Create a list of terms and phrases likely to resonate well with your kids.

A team of communicators from our children's ministry developed the following list to prompt your thinking:

Sin	things we do wrong, bad things we do, no-no's, mistakes, naughty stuff, when we disobey, make bad choices, things we do that make God sad
Punishment	get grounded/time-out/spanking/have to stay in room, consequences, penalty, get in trouble, be disciplined
Crucified	died on a cross because that person was in so much trouble, killed, hurt bad and then died
Savior	forever friend, rescuer, helper, took bad stuff for us, agrees to be in trouble instead of you, took our place, was hurt and killed even though he did nothing wrong
Resurrection	alive again, came back from being dead, didn't stay dead, came back to life
Ask Jesus into your heart	follow Jesus, become a Christian, become best friends with Jesus, start a relationship with Jesus, tell Jesus you're sorry and ask him to always be your friend
Lord or Leader of my life	let Jesus show me the right/best way to live, let Jesus help you make right choices, Jesus helps me do the right things, a guide, have Jesus as the one I follow and obey, someone who will always listen/care/help
Ask for forgiveness	say you're sorry, apologize
Forgiveness	not in trouble anymore
Confess	admit you did wrong, tell what you did
Eternal life	live forever in heaven with Jesus

Now imagine what the gospel message might sound like when using child-centered terms. The following explanation (originally used by a parent in our church as a response to his daughter's question "How do you get to heaven?") will stimulate your imagination:

Do you remember how God can do everything and see everything? Well, that means he can see all the things we do, even the things that aren't nice. He also knows when we are saying stuff that isn't nice, and even when we're not thinking nice things. All of that really disappoints God because he doesn't think it's okay for us to do anything wrong. Can you imagine all the wrong stuff you or I do? No matter if we get caught or not, it means we should be in a lot of trouble. So much trouble that one day when we die, we wouldn't be allowed in heaven. That would be sad, wouldn't it?

But that's where Jesus helps us out. He never did anything wrong, but he still agreed to be in trouble with God for all the things that we did wrong. It's like he agreed to take all the spankings and time-outs for what other people have done. Can you imagine how many that would be? Do you know how he had to do it? He had to actually die hanging on a cross. But he didn't stay dead, which is how he can be with us today. And the real good news is that what he did will count for all the bad things you and I do. All we have to do is ask him to forgive us and to always be our friend, and to help us figure out how to do good stuff. Want to know how to do that?

Susan Shadid, who oversees Promiseland's training program and contributes valuable expertise to curriculum content, suggests adding a reference to joining God's family when explaining the salvation plan. "Children possess a universal longing to belong, so the very real opportunity to be part of a family appeals to many kids," she explains. Consider the potential intrigue that will come to your children when you discuss the other, larger "family" that everyone in your home has an invitation to join.

Consider specific word changes in the language you naturally use to explain prayer, baptism, communion, church attendance, volunteerism, and other common aspects of Christian life.

After you consider new words that will increase kids' comprehension of the gospel message, then turn your attention to other aspects of Christianity and Bible stories that might confuse children. That list may be fairly long. To start, consider specific word changes in the language you naturally use to explain prayer, baptism, communion, church attendance, volunteerism, and other common aspects of Christian life. This isn't an exercise in rewording established doctrine—it's to achieve kid-friendly explanations for important concepts. Then do the same for a Bible story or two.

It's Still His Story and His Timing

Even as I was at work on this chapter, a question came up during one of the morning moments our family spends reading the Bible together. We were partway through Matthew when my daughter asked me about the Roman commander in Matthew 8 whose servant receives long-distance healing from Jesus. "I don't get that story," said seven-year-old Erin. So I offered this explanation:

"The Roman soldier believes Jesus has the power to heal, which means he can make sick people feel better. This soldier even believes that Jesus is so powerful that he can heal anyone just by saying 'Be healed.' This Roman is an important guy, who gives other people orders they have to follow. So he tells Jesus that he believes Jesus has the same ability to give an order—no matter what it is—and it will be done. Even something like healing a sick person. Jesus was pretty impressed that this real important Roman guy believed in Jesus' power to do stuff—which meant the Roman had faith in Jesus. So when we talk about having faith in Jesus, we really mean that we believe in Jesus' power and that he can do anything. Jesus said that because the Roman soldier had lots of faith, he would heal the guy's servant. And you know what? Later on in the Bible, Jesus says if we have that same kind of faith in him, then he'll answer *our* prayers."

And the story gets even better. Erin seemed to understand the concept of faith fairly well, thanks to that story in Matthew 8:5–13. I drew that conclusion when she said, in summary:

"So if faith is believing in Jesus' power, then maybe I should say more prayers to him when I get scared of storms." Imagine how huge her eyes became, and how hard my heart pounded, when the very next day we started reading at verse 23—the story of Jesus calming the storm!

I could not have planned that sequence of stories any better, nor am I foolish enough to think I should try. The same truth applies to modifying our language to share the gospel with kids. We will not consider changing words to fit our expectations of what the gospel should be or what the Bible "ought to" say. We will, though, change the words we use to make God's story, his plan, more accessible to kids. Because the only way a plan has strong appeal is when it's understood.

The plan, of course, is God's rather than ours. Even though we deliver the message, true comprehension and conviction comes solely as a result of the Holy Spirit. To that end, no matter how well we word the gospel, different kids will require different quantities of time to fully understand. Give yours as much as he or she needs.

> Even though we deliver the message, true comprehension and conviction comes solely as a result of the Holy Spirit.

At the start of this chapter, I shared my son Scott's delight when he heard about an incredible, we'll-do-anything-you-want plan in place during amusement park visits every summer. A piece of the story I didn't share earlier is that he waited until the second year to fully take advantage of the plan and order the mountain of ice cream. Similarly, it may take awhile before your child decides he or she is ready to do something about the world's *greatest* plan. And you will want to be ready. Because when that day comes, you don't want to let the opportunity melt away.

Personal Exercises

1. On the chart below, fill in kid-friendly and age-appropriate terms that will connect best with your children:

Sin	
Punishment	
Crucified	
Savior	
Resurrection	
Ask Jesus into your heart	
Lord or Leader of my life	
Ask for forgiveness	
Forgiveness	
Confess	
Eternal life	

2. On one side of a small note card list the four parts of the salvation plan: God, Us, Christ, You and Me. (For some people, adding this as a memo to your PDA might work better than having a physical card.) Next to each point, write a short sentence of explanation. Carry this card so you can refresh your memory prior to any situation in which you might have the chance to share God's story (with kids or adults).

3. Practice explaining the salvation plan with at least two other adults. (If you are reading this book as a husband and wife, you may want to do this together.) Ask for feedback on clarity and kid-friendliness.

CHAPTER 4

The Prayer and Beyond

nticipation built like water collecting behind a dam. Our family had wanted to ride the bumper cars at a local amusement park, but the line stretched so long we decided to keep walking. "We'll come back a little later so we don't waste time waiting," I assured my son. We passed the hours engaged in activities that delivered less fun, knowing that eventually the line would shorten and our decision to delay satisfaction would pay off. To our pleasant surprise, we discovered a unique advantage to small amusement parks—all attractions are scaled down in size, meaning the fear factor is low and so is the minimum height to ride. All, that is, except for one.

Bumper cars deliver a unique flavor of fun. What starts as a group of people stepping into cute little cars painted in bright primary colors quickly changes into twenty-four heavy projectiles intentionally crashing into each other. It's a bump-or-be-bumped experience, and the objective is the harder the better. The world is a different place on the bumper car ride for several reasons.

THE SEVEN WONDERS OF BUMPER CARS

1. For unknown reasons, dads change when they sit in bumper cars and become the roughhousing, out-to-hurt-someone person they don't tolerate back home.

2. Unbelievably, a wad of bubble gum will not short out the electrical grate above the cars — the power source that supplies the current to make everything run.

3. For three minutes, just for fun, mature adults deliberately build up speed for twenty feet and slam cars that carry their entire body weight into cars driven by ten-year-old children.

4. An interesting ride feature is that if the steering wheel is turned far enough the car will move in reverse. This does not work in real automobiles and takes more than three minutes for some people to learn.

5. There's always one passive person who naively tries to avoid contact with other cars, thus becoming a high-priority target for the dads.

6. Total strangers will form unspoken, sinister alliances in less than ten seconds to terrorize that passive person until the ride ends — and it never ends quickly.

7. The ride will be shut down immediately when one is escorted from a bumper car for throwing bubble gum at the electrical grate.

After the crowd thinned, our family arrived at the bumper car line. Common sense told us that our three-year-old daughter was much too young, so she and my wife sat down nearby. That left Scott and me, the boys, to defend the family name on the bumper-car battlefield. Our spirits soared as we approached the turnstile.

Although I felt prepared to encounter and overcome the wonder-filled world we were set to enter, unfortunately we ran into an unexpected problem. The top of Scott's head measured less than an inch short of the minimum height. We experienced shock and awe. Shock at the fact that only one measuring stick in this entire park eliminated Scott—from the ride we most wanted to go on, no less. The awe came after I said, "Awe, c'mon. He's so close!" The high school-aged attendant just shook his head. Mine lowered.

> But despite the presence and influence of moms and dads with God-honoring intentions, every child must decide on his or her own to cross the line of faith.

Then Scott spoke up. "What about you, Dad?" he said. "Aren't you big enough?"

"Of course I am, Buddy," I said, "but I'm not going to just leave you out." (I admit that option did momentarily flash through my mind.)

"No, Dad," he said. "I mean you're big enough to make that guy let me on!"

Don't worry—I didn't try to overpower the hired hand. He was just doing his job. But that experience did help me realize once again that there are some things an adult simply can't do for a child. Obviously, I had no power to make my son tall enough for that ride. He had to do that for himself.

In similar fashion, we can't start our child's personal relationship with Jesus. Oh, we might want to—all parents want the best for their kids. But despite the presence and influence of moms and dads with God-honoring intentions, every child must decide on his or her own to cross the line of faith. And that's the focus of this chapter—helping kids take the crucial step to accept Christ as Lord and Savior. With simple preparation on our parts, we can ensure that the last step doesn't include any major bumps.

HELPING KIDS TAKE THE FINAL STEP

What moment are we preparing for? The one in which your child or mine asks about what he or she needs to do to become a Christian. Of course the question doesn't always sound the same, and the circumstances surrounding it promise to be unpredictable. But the outcome can be incredible, as my friend Carla affirms in a story involving her five-year-old daughter.

> Alyssandra and I had been watching videos about the book of Matthew, and as a result, she had a lot of questions. She wanted to know why people didn't like Jesus. When I explained why and what he stood for, she asked if I believed in Jesus. I told her yes. Then she asked me if I was going to heaven. I told her yes, that I had prayed to accept Christ. I then explained the steps of the prayer.
>
> She said to me, "I love Jesus; I want Jesus to live in my heart. Will you help me pray that prayer?" I was so excited —I had tears in my eyes!
>
> So we prayed together, about eight o'clock at night, driving on a highway on December 14. I still remember the light of the moon shining on her little face as she sat in the backseat.

Carla feels fortunate that she knew how to explain the salvation prayer. And in time, I imagine Alyssandra will feel grateful too. To make the most of any opportunity that might come our way, whether on a highway lit by the moon or in a hallway on the way to breakfast, let's get to work at understanding the prayer. We'll start by looking in the Bible.

Scripture to Guide Our Journey

In Acts 2:37, a large group of people heard the story of Jesus and someone asked the disciples, "Brothers, what shall we do?" Fourteen chapters later, in Acts 16:30, the Roman jailer asked Paul and Silas nearly the same question: "Sirs, what must I do to be saved?" The responses in both situations lay the foundation for how we should help children who ask similar questions.

Acts 2:38 records Peter telling the group to repent. Acts 16:31 shows Paul and Silas responding to the jailer with "Believe in the Lord Jesus." Both examples give clear direction that an internalization of the salvation message needs to take place. To *repent* requires me to personally acknowledge that I've done wrong, while to *believe* starts with a personal conviction that something is true or reliable. And the Bible has more to say about being saved.

Romans 10:9 provides excellent coaching for what a person must do for salvation, "If you confess with your mouth, 'Jesus is Lord,' and believe in your heart that God raised him from the dead, you will be saved." As does Matthew 10:32 (NRSV), "Everyone therefore who acknowledges me before others, I also will acknowledge before my Father in heaven." The same Greek word appears for "confess" and "acknowledge"—with the root word meaning that something is stated. Both these verses point us to the role words play in turning one's life over to Christ.

Combine these four passages (Acts 2:37–38; 16:30–31; Romans 10:9; and Matthew 10:32), and the need for a prayer—something stated—becomes apparent. Some Christ-followers may debate whether or not the prayer must be said aloud for others to hear, but that's not the point. What's truly important for our discussion is that we have the opportunity to help our sons and daughters cross the line of faith if we can assist them in saying a prayer. For simplicity's sake, we'll assume our son or daughter speaks the words.

Words for an A-B-C Salvation Prayer

But what words? Let's go back to Acts to find out. *Repenting of sins* emerges as important, which involves admitting my sins and asking for forgiveness. *Believing on the Lord Jesus* means to understand that he died for my sins and rose again, and that he must become the Lord—or leader—of my life. Not exactly kid-friendly words yet, so let's continue to work on them. If the salvation prayer is to serve as a basic tool that we can use with children, then it should be as easy to remember as A-B-C.

The origin of using A-B-C for the salvation prayer is obscure, but its simplicity is quite evident. Remember those three letters and you can help anyone—young or old—pray to become a Christian.

A—Admit your sins and ask for forgiveness.
B—Believe in Jesus and that he died for your sins.
C—Choose to follow Jesus the rest of your life.

In second grade, Sarah decided she had heard enough about God to make a decision. She vividly remembers the morning when she became a Christian:

> I already knew some stuff about God, and I knew it [following Christ] was an important decision. So I decided to wait until I was older to take that step.
>
> Finally in second grade, I felt like I really understood and wanted to have a relationship with Jesus. The A-B-C prayer just made so much sense to me. I prayed it after hearing an adult describe how she became a Christian; her story was a big deal to me.
>
> The whole day felt like something big just happened.

Something big did happen for Sarah that day, catalyzed by something as simple as A-B-C. Sarah was clearly ready to take the step of praying for salvation, but such clarity isn't always the case. Due to the eternal stakes involved with this prayer, it is important to follow three simple guidelines that address common questions about whether or not a child is ready to enter a relationship with Christ.

Simple Readiness Guidelines

First, make sure your child possesses a genuine, personal desire to pray. When the whole family is together, for instance, pressure to "fit in" can, unfortunately, result in misguided motivation. As can your son's or daughter's desire to please you. Sensitivity to both situations will enable your discernment as to whether or not the Holy Spirit is at work—in a child-sized way, of course. Simply saying a prayer is not what we're after; it must be sincere. And in most cases, one easy question delivered in a gentle tone will reveal the motivation behind why a kid wants to ask Jesus into his or her life: "Can you tell me why you want to do this?"

After posing the question, remain quiet until your child offers a response. If it's no, then review the salvation plan (see chapter 3) and ask questions along the way to create an open dialogue in which the child feels safe to admit any confusion. For example, "Over the last week, have you done anything that you knew was wrong to do?"

Don't discount a child's desire to pray for salvation on more than one occasion.

If she does have a reason for asking Jesus into her life that makes age-appropriate sense, then prompt the child through the A-B-C prayer.

Second, don't discount a child's desire to pray for salvation on more than one occasion. Chris, now a teenager, looks back at his faith journey and appreciates the flexibility and understanding shown by his small group leaders:

> I prayed the A-B-C prayer for the first time in third grade. But the next year, my small group leader explained more concepts about being a Christian, so I decided to pray again. Then my next small group leader showed our group how to put even more parts of following Jesus into motion. He made everything so easy to understand with how he described stuff, so I said the A-B-C prayer again.
>
> My understanding of this commitment grew each year, which is why I kept praying. Life gets more intense each year — especially in sixth grade, so I just wanted to be sure.

Fortunately, no one — especially not his parents — ever gave Chris the sense that what he was doing was wrong or unnecessary. If your child more fully understands salvation this month or this year and wants to pray again, or possibly just wants to be sure about the issue, your guideline is simply to encourage him. I don't find any passage in the Bible that says it is wrong to pray a salvation prayer more than once. Although once is literally enough for eternity, praying more frequently might offer a kid greater comfort and certainty. Especially when life gets intense.

Third, consider age—but don't use age as a reason to dismiss your son's or daughter's desire to start a relationship with Jesus. Psychologist Karen Maudlin says, "God honors the prayers of tender hearts time and time again.... It is safe to say that most children under ten have a hard time conceptualizing a 'life-long' commitment. That doesn't mean [a child's] faith is any less real."[1]

Age will, though, play a distinct role in articulating the prayer.

As much as possible, the words your child prays should be his own—so offer only gentle guidance through the prayer's three portions. However, common sense tells us that the younger the age, the greater your expectation should be for a repeat-after-me prayer rather than for a child's ability to follow your prompt.

> Ideally, you will explain the three components of the prayer, and then your child will tell God what he or she admits, believes, and chooses.

The word "prompt" needs explanation. Ideally, you will explain the three components of the prayer, and then your child will tell God what he or she admits, believes, and chooses. But remembering all three is difficult for someone who hears about this prayer for the first time. That said, explain A and then give the child time to respond before continuing. The following paragraph serves as an example of prompting a child through the A-B-C prayer:

> Okay Lisa, sounds to me like you're ready to start a relationship with Jesus. Let's pray together, and I'll help you know what to say. Here we go.

God, my daughter Lisa wants to start a relationship with Jesus.

Lisa, now it's your turn to go ahead and tell God that you've done wrong stuff and ask him to forgive you ... (pause)

Good job. Now tell him that you really do believe in Jesus, and believe that he died as the punishment for the wrong stuff you've done ... (pause)

Cool. Now tell him that you have decided to follow Jesus the rest of your life ... (pause)

Amen! Way to go Lisa—I love you!

Options on How to Respond

"Lisa" just made the most important decision of her life, one that deserves a deliberate response on your part. First, resist the urge to revisit anything your child said in Admit. Any repercussions—immediate or future—will disrupt her enthusiasm for Jesus, or worse, make her rethink her decision altogether.

Then, consider one or all of the following ideas:

1. Immediately make a big deal about the decision.
   Explode with words of congratulations, high fives,
   a long hug, and any other excitement you can show.
   Purposefully avoid appearing solemn or stoic. As a
   parent, this is likely an incredible answer to your own
   prayers. Witnessing and participating in another person's
   salvation stimulates a feeling that, I believe, is as close
   to the euphoria of heaven as can be experienced in this
   world—especially when that person is your child.
2. Help mark the moment with a gift that shows the date.
   Some parents give a Bible with words of encouragement
   written inside the cover. I know parents who record
   the event in a family journal of extraordinary

accomplishments. My children have their faith affirmed
every time they see the exact dates of their salvations.

3. Ensure that your child owns a Bible he or she can read
   and understand. Scripture acts as God's words to us—a
   major way that he speaks as part of our relationship
   with him. Age plays the key role in deciding which
   version to purchase; any Christian bookstore can
   help you find the most appropriate Bible out of many
   currently on the market.

No doubt a long list of other good ideas exists. The most
important factor with any idea, though, is to give thought
before it's needed so you're ready to act when your child prays.
The moment will evaporate quickly if you do nothing, so
pause briefly right now and consider what you will do if that
big moment arrives soon.

The Bible directs believers to experience baptism as an out-
ward expression of an internal decision to follow Christ. Some
churches baptize people of any age who begin a relationship
with Jesus, while others ask children to wait until a minimum
age to assure their complete understanding. Rather than advo-
cating one approach over another, I suggest that you follow the
discernment of your church's elders. To that end, talk with
your son or daughter about baptism (unless they've already
been baptized)—whether it's an option for that day or some
day in the future. Just be certain that they understand the
meaning of baptism and why Christ-followers throughout the
centuries have participated in this sacrament.

Encourage your son or daughter to continue praying. The
A-B-C prayer demonstrated how to informally talk with God,
so now remind your child that relationships require people to
speak to one another. Serve as a model for how to pray, and
remember to also model listening to God during prayer.

The Right Time — Any Time

You never know what eternal-stakes moment you'll find your-self in, so prepare. God taught me the value of preparation one evening while I worked on developing the original *Leading Kids to Jesus* training course for our children's ministry. I didn't expect a holy moment to arrive when my son, then four years old, opened the door to my office a few minutes before bedtime. But it did. In a moment as quick as a thought, the concepts I had spent hours typing on a keyboard jumped into reality.

As Scotty waited for me to turn off the computer, he spot-ted a century-and-a-half-old five-volume study Bible. "Where did you get those books?" he asked.

"When Great-grandpa Vander Meulen died, Grandma gave me his Bibles," I replied as we walked up the stairs to his bed-room.

"Why did Grandpa V. die?" he asked.

"Well, he lived for a long time, and just got old, I guess," I said.

Scotty pressed on, "Where did he go when he died?"

I paused and reminded myself to think — and breathe!

"Grandpa V. went to heaven," I responded.

"You mean where God and Jesus live?" Scotty countered, clearly showing he was listening in Promiseland.

"Yes."

"Where is heaven?" was the next question he posed, and he really seemed interested to know.

"Well, where do you think it is?"

"It's way up in the sky!" was Scotty's excited response, proud to be adding facts to the conversation. "So Daddy ... how do you get to heaven?"

My pulse raced as I realized what was taking place. Then I gave it my best shot.

"You know how we say you and I are 'buddies'?" I asked. This question referred to the exclusive group the two of us had formed, promising to always be better than best friends.

"Well, to get to heaven you have to decide to be buddies with Jesus forever, which is a real long time. And part of being buddies is that you tell him you're sorry for doing wrong things, and ask him to help you do right things instead. Anyone who is buddies with Jesus gets to go to heaven. And you know what? He would love to hear you tell him you want to live with him someday in heaven."

The pause in his questions seemed to last hours, but was probably less than two seconds. "Do you think they have fire trucks to play with in heaven?"

"Well, what have you learned about God in Promiseland?" I asked.

"God can do anything!" he shouted—his enthusiastic response to that question throughout the previous year.

"Don't you think that if God can do anything, that he probably has the greatest fire trucks ever to play with?!" This was getting fun.

"Yeah! And Daddy, you're buddies with Jesus, right? So you're going to heaven, right?"

"Yeah, Scotty, I sure am."

"Well, do you think we can go out to breakfast all the time when we're in heaven?"

As I shut off the light and sat in his bed with him, I said, "Yeah, I'll bet we probably can." Breakfast enthusiast and bacon lover—just like his dad!

With the lights off, the time had come for prayers before drifting off to sleep. I'll never forget Scott's prayer that night.

"Excuse me God" (I've always loved his casual beginnings to prayers), "you know what? I want to always be buddies with Jesus because I want to live with you in heaven when I die. So let's always be buddies, okay? And I'm sorry when I do bad stuff, okay? And God, can you make sure you have lots of fire trucks? Thanks that I'm buddies with Jesus. Amen!"

As I sat there next to him, I wore both a smile and a tear. A very real spiritual journey was underway. As soon as I heard the familiar heavy breathing, I kissed Scotty's forehead and whispered, "I love you, buddy. And I love you and thank you, Lord." As I quietly made my way out of his dark room, I still had the smile. And I had a real strong feeling that at that same moment, God had one too.

I've had a lot of thrills in life — making two free throws with four seconds left to win a double-overtime basketball game, marrying the woman of my dreams, teaching conferences full of people eager to lead kids to Christ, even riding bumper cars countless times. Yet none compare with the exhilaration I felt that night with my son. And that feeling had nothing to do with what I said; it was all about what he did. Because there are some things kids must do for themselves — and the result is pure joy on earth and a celebration in heaven.

"In the same way, I tell you, there is rejoicing in the presence of the angels of God over one sinner who repents" (Luke 15:10).

Personal Exercises

1. On the back of the note card (or on the PDA memo) you made as a personal exercise following chapter 3, write the letters A, B, and C with a short explanation of each.

2. Practice prompting a partner through an A-B-C prayer. Repeat at least twice.

3. Plan what you will do in response to the moment your child prays for salvation.

CHAPTER 5

The Early Years

'll always remember the first ride my son and I took in the Space Shuttle. Not a real shuttle—an amusement park virtual reality attraction that captured his three-year-old imagination. Even to a thirty-three-year-old, it looked real.

Our cruise of the cosmos aboard this full-scale replica of a NASA shuttle actually began as we stood in line. The detailed decor and believable background noises convinced us that we had stepped into an actual rocket launch center. Prior to the shuttle doors opening, flight control personnel briefed Scott, me, and the staging room filled with fellow astronauts about what to expect on our journey—just like they do at NASA, or so I imagined. After settling into our seats, the multiscreen video and audio experience—complete with choreographed seat jolts and vibrations—delivered a thrilling trip to space and back. So realistic that, despite constant self-reminders that this was merely a movie and simulated experience, a twinge of very real motion sickness hit me. As the shuttle glided through a perfect virtual landing, my excitement returned—this time to get off the ride.

As Scott and I walked away from the faux ship, the fresh air helped me regain my equilibrium. Within a few yards, though, Scott suggested that we stop. Turning back toward the shuttle, we watched the next group of space travelers board.

We continued to watch as more people got in line. And we kept watching, with Scott's eyes glued on the flying machine that towered in front of us.

"Scotty, do you want to ride it again?" I asked, trying to ignore the queasiness that the question prompted.

"No, not really," he responded. We watched awhile longer.

"Buddy, if we're not going to ride it again, why are we standing here?" I asked.

His reason provided me with a memorable line that still makes me smile: "I want to see it take off!"

He thought that the shuttle replica would fire its main engines and blast out of the park. To Scott, the experience had seemed real. All the adults who operated the ride gave instructions for a journey into space, so why wouldn't he believe them?

BELIEF WITHOUT QUESTIONING

That moment illustrated a key truth that Karyn Henley describes in *Child-Sensitive Teaching*: "Young children generally believe what they are told without questioning whether it is true."[1] Fortunately, in the case of Christianity, we have a message based entirely on truth.

In *Teaching Kids about God*, John Trent (et al) offers a similar thought. "Between birth and kindergarten," he writes, "kids are ultimately receptive."[2] Considering the topic we're discussing, can you see the potential presented by your child's natural receptivity?

Clearly, these early years offer an era of opportunity for us to lay a spiritual foundation in our sons and daughters that will someday support a strong faith. The potential payoff of influencing our children during this season of life forms the rationale behind theologian Francis Xavier's comment, "Give me kids until they're seven, and then anyone can have them."[3]

And an unexpected conversation with my daughter demonstrated to me the wisdom behind that statement.

These early years offer an era of opportunity for us to lay a spiritual foundation in sons and daughters that will someday support a strong faith.

Two-year-old Erin loved her dolls. One day, she and I spent an afternoon on the floor of her room with her complete doll family. I was entrusted with the daddy figure, and performed as best I could. She capably took responsibility for the mommy, sister, brother, grandma, grandpa, and two neighbors.

As I tried to stay focused on the pretend world I found myself in, she surprised me with a question: "Daddy, you *lub* Jesus?"

Shocked, I replied, "Of course I do, sweetie."

She proceeded to ask if Mommy (her real one) and brother Scott loved Jesus too. "Sure do," I responded in both cases. Satisfied with the answers, she went back into the doll family fantasy neighborhood.

But eager to stretch this moment out further, I asked her, "Erin, do *you* love Jesus?" and held my breath.

To my surprise—and joy—she said in cool and casual manner, "Yeah, I *lub* Jesus."

As a parent I had a good idea about what prompted our conversation. At home and in our children's ministry program, Erin had heard about loving Jesus and how Jesus loves her. That caused her to decide that she too would "lub Jesus."

A big revelation took place for me that day in my daughter's room: Erin and Jesus had started to form a relationship. At least they had according to what she believed—a belief so strong that she wanted to be sure her mommy, daddy, and brother shared it. A belief so real that she would think it odd for anyone to suggest otherwise. From that point on, the world would have a far more difficult time trying to convince my daughter that a relationship with Jesus is wrong or impossible. Sorry, world. I've been told her stubbornness comes from my side, which for once I'll claim as a compliment. Five years later, her beliefs remain strong—as shown by her words that I shared in a portion of chapter 1 called the Gospel According to Erin.

BELIEF WITHOUT COMPLETE UNDERSTANDING

Of course a world of difference exists between believing something is true and understanding every aspect of it. Yet while God expects us to believe, he never commands his people to have complete understanding. Many of the Bible's faith-filled servants provide us with great examples of this principle. Noah did not understand about the storm front just over the horizon, but he did believe God wanted him to build a boat. Moses had no idea how a bush could burn and not turn into ashes, but he believed God spoke to him through it. The blind man in John 9 believed in the power of Jesus to heal him, but had no idea how it could possibly happen. Without hesitation, he boldly walked before the powerful religious officials and stated the only thing that mattered to him: "One thing I do know. I was blind but now I see!" (verse 25). Belief at any age serves as a strong step toward faith.

A two-year-old can *extend a little piece of her heart to Jesus — a truth that can transform the floor of any family room into an evangelism field.*

Did Erin experience salvation at two? No. At two years old, she did not understand what becoming a Christian means. Years later she would become a "forever friend" with Christ when she sincerely said the A-B-C prayer (discussed in chapter 4). But clearly, a two-year-old *can* extend a little piece of her heart to Jesus—a truth that can transform the floor of any family room into an evangelism field. John Trent (et al)

acknowledges such an opportunity when he says, "It's never too early for God's created people to do the very thing he created them for: have a deep friendship with him."[4] And to that end, the rest of the chapter will examine three areas to focus on if you have children in their early years.

How to Effectively Reach a Young Child
Positively Connect the Child's World to God

Acts 17 tells the story of the apostle Paul's encounter with the people of Athens, including his persuasive words to help them understand God (verses 16–32). Perhaps you've never thought of that scriptural passage from this perspective, but I suggest you can mimic his approach to reach out to your children.

Specifically, Paul noticed that Athens was a city full of worship idols—including an altar "to an unknown god" (Acts 17: 23). The apostle proceeded to connect the world of the Athenians to the true God, when he said, "What you worship as something unknown I am going to proclaim to you" (verse 23). From Paul's example we learn that creating a connection between a person's actual environment and the Lord can serve as a strong starting point to reach someone to whom God seems unknown. Such as young kids.

The rest of Paul's speech in Acts 17 appeals to religious people and philosophers, so let's take his lead as we build an appropriate approach to use with children. That approach begins with understanding an important, basic requirement that precedes any relationship with God—a person must have awareness of God. In Romans 10:14 (NRSV), Paul describes the importance of this concept and the inherent responsibility it places on believers: "But how are they to call on one in whom they have not believed? And how are they to believe in one of whom they have never heard? And how are they to hear without someone to proclaim him?"

Proclaim the Lord to our young kids? Paul's words lay out an interesting challenge to parents with very young children, especially moms and dads who may believe that the littlest of kids lacks the ability to comprehend God. That perception needs to change.

In *Child-Sensitive Teaching*, Karyn Henley describes the importance of introducing our babies—yes, babies—to God in very simple ways.[5] To do this, she says, we must create an association between our kids' sensory experiences and God. The result can be a strong connection between their world and the one who created the world, even when they don't yet know the meanings of words used.

Making connection points is simple. As an infant experiences joy, rest, peace, warmth, or wonder, then talk to that child with clear emphasis on God's role in what's taking place. These opportunities appear frequently for parents, and require no effort past a few well-timed words.

For instance, while providing comfort to a fussy child, softly tell her, "I'm here for you, and God is always here for you." Karyn Henley suggests telling a baby enjoying a banana, "God made this banana."[6] While spending time holding a little one in a rocking chair, sing songs to him that clearly and frequently use the names God and Jesus. If, like me, you have the vocal talent of an injured farm animal, then remember to sing softly. And smile.

Over time, little minds will remember the name of the Almighty and the feeling experienced as they heard that name. An automatic, internal connection between God and a warm hug, tasty snack, soothing voice, and bright eyes gives kids a giant head start toward a future friendship with the Lord. Modify the thought "I must take care of my baby" to "I will introduce my baby to God!" You'll join others who share this conviction and practice.

Churches in increasing numbers now understand that deliberate ministry must replace childcare in the nursery area. Just ask author and pastor Jack Hayford at The Church on the Way in Los Angeles, California. In his book *Blessing Your Children*, he says, "We train even the nursery workers to recognize the power of their personal touch on the babies in their care. Those who are part of that ministry are trained to believe in and exercise spiritual vitality and love in a way that can impart life to their young charges. By prayer, singing, and speaking tender words—even sitting and rocking an infant—an infusion of the life of the Holy Spirit can flow from these workers into that baby."[7]

Clearly Communicate God's Truth and Love

At some point in our adult lives, you and I inherit the habit of complicating everything. We may discard a belief that God said, "Let there be light; and there was light," in favor of speculation about a big bang. Rainbows become a refracted light spectrum illuminated from airborne water molecules instead of an artistic reminder of a divine promise. And the thought of avoiding leaf-raking duties by cutting down that big maple in the backyard replaces the wonder that God creates beautiful trees. Young kids need us to reject this unfortunate inheritance.

> The recipe for success includes common and uncomplicated ingredients that all of us possess—simple thoughts, plain words, and short sentences.

As children move out of the infant stage and into ages two and three, a new opportunity emerges to usher them closer to God: to verbally communicate God's truth and love in tiny, bite-sized pieces. The recipe for success includes common and uncomplicated ingredients that all of us possess—simple thoughts, plain words, and short sentences.

In similar fashion to "God made this banana," parents can casually declare truths about God to a little one in terms of the world the child sees or experiences. Dr. James Dobson says, "Even at three years of age, a child is capable of learning that the flowers, the sky, the birds and even the rainbow are gifts from God's hand."[8] With their fresh capability to learn, kids eagerly soak up explanations about a world they long to understand. Let's look at a practical example.

The team in our ministry's three-year-old area taught a summer unit titled "God made the world." A rather big concept for sure, so each week we examined a piece of God's creation that someone aged three could readily understand. The week I served as a small group leader, we explored the topic "God created the animals."

The large group lesson explained in very simple words that God created animals in Genesis 1, followed by a pretend trip through the zoo where we repeated the words of truth, "God made the animals." Then small group time began.

As we munched a snack—animal crackers, of course—we took turns saying the name of an animal, and then stating that God made that creature. I added the fun twist of letting each child act like the animal he or she named. For example, on my turn I got on my hands and knees and growled real loud. After someone correctly guessed "a bear," we all said together, "God made the bears!" As it turned out, our group had lots of bears.

After going around the circle twice, the group had learned the lesson cold, but the parents had not yet come from big church to pick up their kids. With a few extra minutes at my disposal, I showed the group—to their amazement—that I could balance an empty paper cup (it previously held my crackers) on my head. No, the lesson plan did not include the cup trick; extra fun was its only purpose. As the parents started to come into the room, I quickly took the cup off my head and passed out the take-home sheets.

When Julio's father approached the group, Julio stood up with a huge smile on his face and said, "Dad, guess what I learned today!" At the same time, he started to raise his paper cup. "Oh no, Julio," I thought, "don't put your cup on your head!"

But then, to my relief, Julio stated loudly and proudly, "God made the animals!" Yes, he remembered the right thing from our time together. As a parent, you walk through plenty of opportunities to teach this lesson—and similar truths about God—to your son or daughter. Think of all the times you see animals, plants, stars, and other evidence of creation to which you can draw your child's attention. What matters most is that you look for chances and slow down when one arrives.

I watched a little boy walk away who believed he had figured out a piece of this world because he knew who made the animals—God. This lesson worked with Julio because it communicated a simple truth using plain words in a short sentence. And it teaches us, who are parents, the value of choosing words deliberately and looking for opportunities to share them.

What length is short enough? Years of experience in our ministry show four words or less to be an effective guideline. Sentences limited to that length can efficiently communicate God's truth and love, with increased odds that a child will remember the words and have the ability to say them on his or her own.

So pause for a moment and consider several four-word, simple statements of God's truth that your two- or three-year-old will understand:

- God made the animals.
- God made the sky.
- God will help me.
- The Bible is true.

The list could go on for many pages. To simplify the application of this tool, look around the environment in which you spend time with your kids. Toys or stuffed animals, picture books, your yard, or a park—all can prompt opportunities. Speaking these words with our kids will turn what might seem as idle playtime into ideal moments to offer insight about God.

Be sure to include statements about love on your list. You will share an incredible gift with your young child when she hears you, the person she likely trusts most, talk about *your* love for Jesus and Jesus' love for you. Just remember to keep it simple and short so that your daughter can repeat the words, if she chooses to: "Jesus loves me," "Jesus loves you," or even "I *lub* Jesus." What an incredible opportunity we have to give our kids the most important words in life before doubt, skepticism, or complications ever exist!

Actively Reinforce the Message

Apart from our spoken words, actions also play key roles in communicating about God. Imagine the love expressed when you pick up a crying child to provide comfort—measured by how that act makes him feel. John Trent (et al) says, "As you hold them, love them, feed them, and keep them warm, you establish that their world is good and safe. In time, as you tell them that God loves them and looks after them, they make the connection between your loving behaviors and God's active love for them."[9] Those behaviors begin with newborns and need to continue as kids grow.

In his book *The Wonder of Girls*, Michael Gurian says, "If a father finds time to cuddle, listen to, toss in the air, dance with, run alongside, coach, comfort, and protect his daughter, he will give her the gift of life."[10] What starts as hours rocked in your arms can continue as meaningful, life-giving moments in those same arms as you both grow older.

How does providing comfort, attention, or affection qualify as communicating about God's love? Easy. When a child sees a really big person (all parents are really big to kids!) come down to his level to engage with him, that kid feels a sense of value. The thought "I must be important" goes through his subconscious mind. And if a child believes he has value in the eyes of big people, the child moves closer to a belief that God

values him. The leap to "God loves me" becomes an easier step to take. Jesus taught extensively on this concept, and he did it without the need for words. His method deserves our focused attention.

Jesus put his hands on children to bless them. "Then little children were being brought to him in order that he might lay his hands on them and pray. The disciples spoke sternly to those who brought them; but Jesus said, 'Let the little children come to me, and do not stop them; for it is to such as these that the kingdom of heaven belongs.' And he laid his hands on them and went on his way" (Matthew 19:13–15 NRSV). He could have simply stood and prayed in the direction of the kids, but he knew the powerful role touch plays in communication with children.

Or imagine the love that lepers felt when Jesus physically touched them. These afflicted people, considered unclean and unhealthy by the rest of society, likely had no other person come even close to them. But Christ knew the potential to communicate a divine love through touch. The contact may have been brief with some, but the power of those moments changed people, probably even those who watched. The impact of Jesus' willingness to make contact with lepers receives an underscore when Matthew begins his numerous descriptions of Christ's miracles with the account of a cleansed leper (see Matthew 8:1–4).

I witnessed firsthand the power of touch while I served in a volunteer role that involved helping a wheelchair-confined boy participate in our ministry, despite his physical challenges. One Sunday morning, as we said our good-byes, he looked like he wanted me to hug him. I had never hugged him to that point, and didn't know how. I feared I might somehow hurt him. But I bent over anyhow, reached my hands around him as best as I could, and hugged him. He hugged me tight and for a long time. Finally, with my back starting to hurt, I stood up. "That was some hug!" I said.

He replied, "Not many people want to hug me."

Time for another confession: Hugging is an act outside my comfort zone when it involves anyone other than my wife and our two kids. But I still feel an uncomfortable lump in my throat when I consider that too many Sundays passed by before I gave that young boy a hug around his shoulders. I must avoid any assumption that kids feel God's love elsewhere in life, and I urge you to do the same. Especially with your own kids.

I remember the specific moment when I committed to break out of my no-hugging comfort zone. My dad and I attended a large men's retreat soon after my son's birth. During a session that focused on helping men express love, the speaker challenged all fathers and sons in the audience to hug each other and say, "I love you." The two of us sat frozen for an awkward second.

"Is he going to do it?" I wondered. The next second went by.

Then a thought flashed through my mind: "What about *you*? Will *you* do it?"

Another second clicked past.

My dad's love for me, and mine for him, was never in question. Expressing that love, though, required an untrained muscle to flex. Yet another second was now gone.

The thought returned: "What about *you*?" The time to act had arrived.

As if choreographed, we simultaneously hugged. During that long embrace I promised God that my children would feel and hear of my love so often that they would laugh at the idea that I once struggled in this area. I would do my best to shorten the distance between the idea of a heavenly father's love and what they receive from their dad on earth. With the hug for my wheelchair-bound charge three years later, I was able to extend that commitment beyond my family circle.

BUILD A STRONG FOUNDATION

Every child develops an understanding of love (good or bad), which will serve as a foundation to support future spiritual beliefs. When a child knows love, many Christian concepts will begin to make sense. Why did God send his only begotten son? Because he so *loved* the world. As Mother Teresa once said, "Love and faith go hand in hand."[11] As parents, we can determine that foundation's strength—which leads every parent to a critical question: Will your child learn about love from you—and how? If you've wondered how best to start putting the information presented in this chapter into practice, answering that question is it.

When we positively connect a young son's or daughter's world to God, clearly communicate God's truth and love, and actively reinforce the message, we help our child move closer to a relationship with Jesus. Sometimes steps along the way are large and sometimes they're small. Regardless of the stride length or footprint size, every step is important because when we share God's truth and love we pave the way for future spiritual development. Peter writes of the desire to see people "grow up in ... salvation" once they "have tasted that the Lord is good" (1 Peter 2:3). We *can* give kids in their early years a little taste—one that will grow into a real hunger in the not-so-distant future.

Personal Exercises

1. List several simple, four-word statements in each of the following categories:

   • Who God is

   • What God does

   • Things we see that remind us of God

   • Descriptions of God's love

2. Write a note to your son or daughter that describes your love for him or her. Read the note to your child often, followed by a long hug.

CHAPTER 6

What If I Don't
Have a Story?

To squeeze the most fun from your amusement park dollar, arrive before the gates open. Veteran visitors know the first hour or two offer the most fun for a simple reason—fewer people. And that means less time spent waiting in lines and more time enjoying the rides.

One summer morning, our family joined the early birds outside the main entrance of one of our favorite parks. We purchased tickets and positioned ourselves near the turnstiles, anticipating the moment we could rush inside to our favorite attractions. As we watched the clock, park workers mingled among the crowd, shouting reminders that seemed silly to me.

"Please make sure to have your ticket out."

"Everyone needs a ticket."

"Nobody gets in without a ticket."

I wondered why they felt the need to remind us of something so basic. Of course everyone would need a ticket. (Just to be safe, though, I checked to make sure I still held four of them in my possession.) The gates soon opened, and our line began to thread people single file into the park. What happened next amazed me. A young man in front of us didn't have a ticket! Instead, he handed the attendant a coupon for free admission.

"I'm sorry, sir," the ticket taker said. "First, you must have a ticket to get in. And second, the coupon is good for a free admission only when you purchase another ticket at full price."

I counted our tickets for the sixth time in less than five minutes—just to make sure I would not share this young man's embarrassment. He learned that those announcements were not so silly after all; if you go to the admission gate without a ticket, you won't get in. You can offer a coupon. You can show a credit card. You can wave a wad of one-hundred-dollar bills at the attendant. But only a purchased ticket will get you through the gate.

Picture yourself in a similar story.

You drive to an amusement park, get out of your car, and head to the admission gate. While in line, you hear that you need a ticket. So you approach the ticket window, and ask for one. The attendant tells you the price, and you gasp. Realistic story so far.

Now imagine that the amount required far surpasses all the money you'll earn in a lifetime. You stand there dumbfounded, not knowing what to do. Your only option is to get out of line. Or is it?

As you stand in the ticket line bewildered, someone calls out to you. You've heard the voice before, but this time you respond. This person wants to pay for your ticket! All you need to do is accept his generosity. In fact, he seems to be making the offer to everyone. So you finally enter the park and wonder why anyone would turn down such an offer.

Once inside the park, you look back toward the people who remain outside the gates. You tell several folks that they should take advantage of the free ticket offer. "It's the only way to get in, it's free," you explain, "and I did it!" The people who listen believe what you say because your words come from actual experience. They get tickets and join you inside the park.

But you also notice a few people still outside the gate telling others about the need for a ticket and the generous man's offer. These folks fail to convince anyone because they lack credibility. Who would follow the advice of someone who has yet to take advantage of this remarkable proposition?

An obvious analogy to accepting Jesus' free gift of grace, right? Of course it is. The "admission price" of a relationship with God surpasses anything you or I can pay, so Jesus paid it for us by dying on the cross. So how much does all this ticket talk relate to helping kids become Christians?

A lot. Because we, as parents, can talk with kids about Jesus authentically only when we have a relationship with Christ. And that qualifier presents an issue for us to consider.

Research by George Barna concludes that "adults who say they are Christian but have never made a profession of faith in Jesus Christ represent almost half of all people attending Christian churches in the U.S."[1] So a large number of people who participate in church have never truly crossed the line of faith—they hang around the park entrance, but never accept the ticket to go inside.

We can assume that several of those individuals are parents. And many of them might have discussions with their kids about faith in Jesus. Some may even read this book, which is why I included this chapter. This one-half of adults in church might even include you. If so, relax. You've done nothing wrong; you just have more distance to travel on your spiritual journey before you recognize a personal need to accept Christ's invitation to a relationship.

That relationship could be as close as the end of this chapter. So let's get personal.

YOUR TICKET

In Acts 2:39, Peter describes the offer of salvation this way: "The promise is for you and your children and for all who are far off—for all whom the Lord our God will call." Notice the order—you first, then your children, followed by everyone else.

How certain are you that you have a ticket? Many people struggle with an honest answer.

Donald Cole, pastor for the Moody Broadcast Network, said the most common question asked by callers to his radio program, even those who consider themselves Christians, is "whether they can be saved and *know it.*"[2] But although wrestling with such certainty appears to be fairly common, keep in mind that your answer to the question carries personal, eternal implications.

> How certain are you that you have a ticket? Many people struggle with an honest answer.

In his book *The Purpose Driven Life*, Rick Warren says, "From the Bible we can surmise that God will ask us two crucial questions: First, 'What did you do with my Son, Jesus Christ?'

God won't ask about your religious background or doctrinal views. The only thing that will matter is, did you accept what Jesus did for you and did you learn to love and trust him?" Rick predicts God's second question will be equally compelling: "'What did you do with what I gave you?' What did you do with your life—all the gifts, talents, opportunities, energy, relationships, and resources God gave you?"[3]

Many parents will accurately point to their work as a mother or father as part of a response to God's second question. A clear, solid answer for the first question, though, will prove difficult for some of those very same folks.

So for the sake of certainty, let's double-check our tickets.

To get the most out of this chapter, try not to react too quickly to challenges concerning your personal faith. We'll find that those challenges spring out of an Old Testament instruction directed toward moms and dads. After we take a fresh look at this important piece of parental advice, we'll consider what a relationship with God is, and just as importantly, what it is not.

OLD TESTAMENT INSTRUCTION

> These commandments that I give you today are to be upon your hearts. Impress them on your children. Talk about them when you sit at home and when you walk along the road, when you lie down and when you get up. Tie them as symbols on your hands and bind them on your foreheads. Write them on the doorframes of your houses and on your gates.
>
> Deut. 6:6–9

The Bible contains passages that are difficult to fully understand, but this is not one of them. Clearly, parents own the primary responsibility to educate their kids about God. Not the church. And definitely not the "let them figure out faith on their own" plan. God's clear expectation is that you and I will frequently talk to our own children about him. The purpose of this book is to help us do that well. The verse immediately before this instruction, though, plays a key role in our ability to have meaningful conversations.

> Love the Lord your God with all your heart and with all your soul and with all your strength.
>
> Deut. 6:5

This command appears immediately before the parental directive, which I doubt is a coincidence. We can consider verse five a divine prerequisite. In other words, prior to talking with your children about God, make sure you are in a significant relationship with God.

The phrase "in a significant relationship with God" deserves clarification. Many people lack this clarity and don't even realize it. I, however, have firsthand experience with this shortcoming.

As I mentioned earlier, at twenty-nine I learned the important difference between knowing information about God and knowing that I have a relationship with Christ. I believed sin is wrong, but I needed to believe that *my* sins were wrong. I believed Christ died on the cross, but I needed to believe that he died for *me*. I believed he offers forgiveness for sins to all people, but I had to believe that *I* needed that forgiveness. All my knowledge about God became personal belief—a conviction so strong that it compelled me to accept Jesus' gift of grace and then commit the rest of my life to an active relationship with him.

All of this took place long after I had consistently attended church throughout my childhood. I literally sat in the house of God every seven days for many years, surrounded by God's Word and good people. As a kid and as a young adult, I stood only one clear salvation explanation away from the possibility of giving my life to Jesus. Unfortunately, that explanation never came. That still happens today with people who actively attend church for years.

At twenty-nine I learned the important difference between knowing information about God and knowing that I have a relationship with Christ.

More recently, I volunteered for five years in our church's evangelism ministry. Among its many responsibilities, our team read the written testimonies of all adults registered for baptism. What a privilege! We frequently pored over stories from individuals who attended church for years and even served as ministry volunteers. Inevitably, each story described a life-changing moment that brought clarity and awareness about that person's need for a savior. Everybody's journey to faith took different turns, but each one ended in a similar place—Admitting sins, Believing Christ died for those sins, and Choosing to follow him (not surprisingly, the components of the A-B-C prayer!). These stories confirmed that church attendance and involvement sometimes precedes a personal relationship with Jesus. And that's fine—as long as the relationship eventually gets underway.

GOD'S NUDGING

God has the ability to communicate with us in countless ways, one of which is to simply nudge a person and then wait for a response. He asked Abraham (Genesis 12) to sacrifice his son Isaac, and then waited to see what would happen. He lit a bush on fire near Moses (Exodus 3), and then waited to see if the flames would catch Moses' attention. He repeatedly woke up a young boy named Samuel by calling out the lad's name (1 Samuel 3), and then patiently waited for Samuel's response. Today, God still nudges people—even those who do not yet know him. And he still waits for their responses.

Is it possible that throughout chapter 2, while we focused on writing and refining your story of faith, you realized you don't have one? In chapter 3 did the salvation plan—worded for kids—make sense to you in ways it never has before? Or in chapter 4 did you read about a prayer (A-B-C) that you have yet to say?

If your heart whispered "yes" to any of these questions, then maybe God has nudged you. And maybe that prompt will point you to an honest realization that you still need to take faith's ultimate step—"confess with your mouth, 'Jesus is Lord,' and believe in your heart that God raised him from the dead" (Romans 10:9). While your answer may be forming, I repeat my request that you resist any reaction or firm conclusion for just a bit longer.

The purpose of this book is to help parents talk clearly with kids about Jesus. So with that same spirit, let's put words to truths that offer clarity about Christianity to adults. Although Christians typically go to Sunday services, attending church or other religious activities does not make someone a Christian. Although many Christians invest their time and talents serving God, volunteering at church does not make someone a Christian. Nor does knowing the Bible well. Or even being a really good person. C. S. Lewis once described a key point in his journey toward authentic faith: "I have just passed on from believing in God to definitely believing in Christ—in Christianity."[4]

Personal Question 1—What Would Jesus Say about You? What about you? The predictable question is to ask whether you have a relationship with Christ. But a more striking question to ponder is this: Would *Jesus* say that you are in a relationship with him? He testifies to the importance of your answer in Matthew 7:23: "Then I will tell them plainly, 'I never knew you. Away from me.'" Good-intentioned people will seek to enter heaven based on their knowledge of Christ—or maybe based on church attendance or involvement—only to be turned away because Christ did not truly know them. So what would Jesus say right now about you? Take a break from reading to let your heart dance with that question for a while.

During a recent breakfast meeting, my friend Dave served up a summary of his spiritual journey: "I knew a lot of verses while growing up. But my life didn't change until I figured out that God isn't just on the pages of the Bible; he is beside me." And that change of location—from printed page to personal presence—makes a world of difference because it begs a response.

Personal Question 2—Have You Responded? Shane Claibourne, a street missionary in Philadelphia who is also a compelling speaker, offers a challenging perspective on Jesus' words in the Bible by asking: "What if he really meant this stuff?"[5] Assuming that Jesus was serious about what he said, your life and mine ought to show evidence of his words' impact. Has that happened? While you read these words from Jesus, let yourself wonder about the impact they should make on your life:

> *"I am the way and the truth and the life. No one comes to the Father except through me."*
>
> John 14:6

> *"Seek first his kingdom and his righteousness."*
>
> Matthew 6:33

"I have come that they may have life, and have it to the full."

John 10:10

"I have told you this so that my joy may be in you and that your joy may be complete."

John 15:11

"Love the Lord your God with all your heart and with all your soul and with all your mind. This is the first and greatest commandment."

Matthew 22:37–38

"Come, follow me."

Luke 18:22

To authentically lead your child into a relationship with Christ requires you to be in such a relationship first. You can only give that which you have. And if something inside you has started to stir, pause from reading right now and respond to God. As you learned in chapter 5, it's as easy as A-B-C (Admit, Believe, Choose).

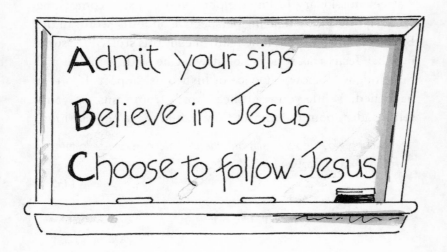

STILL HOLDING OUT?

For some people, the hardest part of becoming a Christian is to escape from underneath their own pride, and to humbly tell Christ they want to start a relationship with him. Especially if others assume they already are Christians—that they've already taken this step. If this has been the case with you, it's not a problem. People figure out their need for Jesus at different paces and at different times in life. And sometimes that time comes as a surprise.

Legendary basketball coach John Wooden once said, "When I was baptized, I really hadn't accepted Christ. I thought I had, but I hadn't."[6] Coach Wooden is but one of many people who understand a truth articulated by Rick Warren in *The Purpose Driven Life*: "Baptism doesn't make you a member of God's family, only faith in Christ does that."[7]

That same, sometimes surprising, truth applies to other ceremonies and rituals as well. In the Bible, God says our hearts are what he desires most: "To love him with all your heart, with all your understanding and with all your strength, and to love your neighbor as yourself is more important than all burnt offerings and sacrifices" (Mark 12:33).

Good news awaits when you arrive at the realization that you need to respond: God won't be surprised! He's expecting you. He's waited your whole life for you to come to him. That wait has been shorter for some people than for others, which actually can introduce its own unique challenge.

Statistics show that most Christians began their relationship with Jesus by age thirteen.[8] And at that age, "What did I have to repent from? Hitting my sister?" asks former Moody Bible Institute president Joe Stowell in reference to his childhood salvation.[9] Because the life change resulting from a childhood commitment may have been less than dramatic, the memory of that decision might prove difficult to recall many years later. That's okay. Remember that Scripture tells us that kids *can* start a relationship with Jesus—the passionate belief that serves as this book's foundation!

If you have a cloudy memory of your childhood decision to become a Christian, spend a few moments considering modified versions of this chapter's two personal questions. First, what would Jesus list as specific differences your faith in him has made throughout various time periods in your life? Second, what choices do you make today as a result of your belief as a Christ-follower? *When* you made the decision to follow Jesus matters little compared with what you do *now* with that faith.

> Because the life change resulting from a childhood commitment may have been less than dramatic, the memory of that decision might prove difficult to recall many years later. That's okay.

And finally, let's acknowledge one last challenge that sometimes creates confusion. Many people initially misinterpret God's nudge to them. Some take it as a directive to try harder to be a good person—one who doesn't lie, cheat, steal, or curse—and they spend life frustrated with their failures. Or they might reason that the good they do outweighs the bad, and hope that God knows how to calculate an average. Some believe God wants them to perform well on a divine grading curve—that they only need to score better than most people. Others feel they've answered the Lord's call when they acquiesce to a spouse's, parent's, or friend's wishes to clean up their lives. C. S. Lewis once said, "We must not suppose that even if we succeeded in making everyone nice we should have saved their souls. A world of nice people, content in their own niceness, looking no further, turned away from God, would be just as desperately in need of salvation as a miserable world—and might even be more difficult to save."[10] Still others believe that God calls them to obey a multitude of rules, doctrines, and dogma that religious institutions expect—or possibly require. That belief, shared by way too many people, creates spiritual busyness that unfortunately drives many people away from God.

These misinterpretations—being really good, being relatively good, behaving for those watching, or immersing oneself in rigid religion—miss the mark because they involve judgment by other people. Complication constantly arises from human expectations for how you and I should live because we can never be good enough by these standards. God offers a simpler plan.

God wants you and me to relate directly with him on a *personal* level—one that requires no one else's involvement. Other people's wishes, desires, and directives are superfluous. What matters is that you and I can honestly say, "I'm a Christian because I'm in a relationship with Christ." That's all that counts.

MOVING INTO A TRUE RELATIONSHIP WITH CHRIST

For a year shy of three decades, I labeled myself a Christian for a variety of reasons other than the right one. My family attended a Christian church, and I became a member. I lived in the United States, which is a Christian country, right? I even owned a Bible and knew several of its stories.

Had I sat through training or read a book on how to lead kids to Christ, I might even have come up with a story of how I became a Christian—not with any ill intent, just out of confusion and a lack of understanding the truth about a relationship with Jesus. A feeling of discomfort undoubtedly would have accompanied my story, though, because it would have lacked authenticity. Fortunately, I eventually moved away from such self-deception and into a true relationship with Christ.

Now that you've finished reading this chapter, I pray that you are confident in what Jesus would say about you, based on your response to him. With that faith, you can feel great about your story—whether it involves events from years past, or just the last twenty minutes. Regardless of when it happened, you have an authentic story to tell your children about how you came to possess life's most valuable ticket.

Personal Exercises

1. Write a letter to Jesus that describes the relationship you and he share, and the difference he has made in your life. If this exercise seems at all difficult, reread this chapter.

2. If you have made a decision to accept Jesus' offer of salvation during the course of reading this chapter, go back to chapter 2 and reconstruct your story to include this new, important detail.

A Final Word

Five years ago, my wife and I spent Valentine's Day meeting with oncologists, a visit that included my first CT scan. Seven days earlier a doctor had found an advanced melanoma tumor on my arm.

Needless to say, I didn't sleep well that night. Previously unthinkable questions raced through my mind. None were the "Why me?" type; rather, I mostly wondered and prayed about my six- and three-year-old children. "If I'm not around, who will teach Scott how to shoot a jump shot? Who will coach him into manhood? Who will hold onto Erin as she learns to ride a bike? And who will walk her down the aisle one day?" Yet all of those questions seemed trivial next to my biggest concern. "Who will talk to them about God and Jesus?" I queried and pleaded with God into the early morning hours until exhaustion carried me off to sleep.

Fortunately I've passed the half-decade point of my cancer adventure, but I frequently revisit that big question. And I always come up with the same answer: "Me." I believe that my February sleepless night—spent wrestling with questions that lacked clear answers—filled me with a resolve that provided oft-needed strength along my journey to good health (which I fully enjoy today). Along the way I learned that when you believe your days are numbered, you determine to make them count.

In practical terms, every time my wife or I have a spiritual conversation with our children, we do so with a deep determination to make the most of the opportunity. We start by deliberately talking with Scott and Erin in a manner they'll understand, using the concepts you've read in this book and giving it our best. Of course we make our share of goofs, but we genuinely believe every discussion counts.

Bring your children's faces to mind for a moment. I believe that you, and every parent, face the same question as I did: Who will talk with my children about God and Jesus? Easy question, right? Then set this book down, go have a conversation, and give it your best. Because the answer your children need—and the person God has selected to step up to the task—is this book's final word: You.

Endnotes

INTRODUCTION

1. George Barna, *Transforming Children into Spiritual Champions* (Ventura, Calif.: Regal, 2003), 33.

2. James Strong, *Strong's Comprehensive Concordance of the Bible*, #5043 (Iowa Falls, Iowa: World Bible Publishers), 70.

3. James Dobson, response received from Focus on the Family website, *www.family.org* (July 8, 2004).

4. Joseph M. Stowell, *Why It's So Hard to Love Jesus* (Chicago: Moody Publishers, 2003), 90.

5. Billy Graham, quoted from the Billy Graham Evangelistic Association website, *www.billygraham.org* (August 4, 2004).

6. C. S. Lewis, *God in the Dock*. Walter Hooper, ed. (Grand Rapids, Mich.: Eerdmans, 1970), 115.

7. Reggie Joiner, "Dream" (General session, Promiseland Conference, Willow Creek Association, South Barrington, Ill, 2005).

8. Ibid.

CHAPTER 1 — COMMUNICATING WITH KIDS

1. Suzette Haden Elgin, *The Gentle Art of Communicating With Kids* (Mississauga, Ontario, Canada: John Wiley & Sons, Inc., 1996), 9.

2. Red Auerbach quoted in Dr. John C. Maxwell, "Playing Over Their Heads," *Leadership Wired*, 7 no. 4 (3/12/04): *www.injoy.com* (March 12, 2004).

3. George Barna, *Transforming Children into Spiritual Champions* (Ventura, Calif.: Regal, 2003), 34.

CHAPTER 2 — SHARE YOUR STORY

1. Bill Hybels quoted in David Staal, "Mission Possible," *Children's Ministry Magazine* 12, September/October 2002, 68.

2. Bill Hybels, "Walking across the Room" (New Community message, Willow Creek Community Church, South Barrington, Ill., January 2004).

3. Eugene Ehrlich and Marshall DeBruhl, *The International Thesaurus of Quotations*, 2nd ed. (New York: HarperCollins, 1996), 649.

4. George Barna, *Transforming Children into Spiritual Champions* (Ventura, Calif.: Regal, 2003), 86.

CHAPTER 3 — SHARE GOD'S STORY

1. Craig Jutila, "The 'C' of Character" (General session 1, Purpose Driven Children's Ministry Conference, Saddleback Church, Lake Forest, Calif., April 2004).

CHAPTER 4 — THE PRAYER AND BEYOND

1. Karen L. Maudlin, "On the Family Front," *Christian Parenting Today*, (Winter 2003), 54.

CHAPTER 5 — THE EARLY YEARS

1. Karyn Henley, *Child-Sensitive Teaching*. (Cincinnati, Ohio: Standard, 1997), 43.

2. John T. Trent, Rick Osborne, and Kurt Bruner, *Teaching Kids about God: An Age-by-Age Plan for Parents of Children from Birth to Age Twelve* (Wheaton, Ill.: Tyndale, 2003), 5.

3. Francis Xavier quoted by Adrian Rogers, *Future for the Family*, Love Worth Finding website, *www.lwf.org* (January 27, 2003).

4. Trent, Osborne, and Bruner, *Teaching Kids about God*, 21.

5. Henley, *Child-Sensitive Teaching*, 37.

6. Ibid.

7. Jack W. Hayford, *Blessing Your Children: How You Can Love the Kids in Your Life* (Ventura, Calif.: Regal, 2002), 49.

8. James Dobson, *Bringing Up Boys* (Wheaton, Ill.: Tyndale, 2001), 248.

9. Trent, Osborne, and Bruner, *Teaching Kids about God*, 13.

10. Michael Gurian, *The Wonder of Girls* (New York: Pocket Books, 2002), 157.

11. Jose Luis Gonzales-Balado, *Mother Teresa, In My Own Words* (New York: Barnes and Noble, 1996), 34.

Chapter 6 — What If I Don't Have a Story?

1. George Barna "Number of Unchurched Adults Has Nearly Doubled Since 1991," Barna Update, Barna Research Group, *www.barna.org* (May 24, 2004).

2. C. Donald Cole, *How to Know You're Saved* (Chicago: Moody Publishers, 1988), 10.

3. Rick Warren, *The Purpose-Driven Life* (Grand Rapids, Mich.: Zondervan, 2002), 34.

4. Wayne Martindale and Jerry Root, *The Quotable Lewis*, #242 (Wheaton, Ill.: Tyndale, 1989), 120.

5. Shane Claiborne, "Faith for the 21st Century: Loving the Overlooked" (Axis weekend message, Willow Creek Community Church, South Barrington, Ill., 2001).

6. John Wooden, *Coach Wooden One-on-One* (Ventura, Calif.: Regal, 1996), Day 49.

7. Warren, *Purpose-Driven Life*, 120.

8. George Barna, *Transforming Children into Spiritual Champions* (Ventura, Calif.: Regal, 2003), 18.

9. Joseph M. Stowell, quoted in email message to author from Moody Bible Institute, November 11, 2004.

10. Wayne Martindale and Jerry Root, *The Quotable Lewis*, #1313, 523.

Making Your Children's Ministry the Best Hour of Every Kid's Week

Sue Miller with David Staal

Promiseland is Willow Creek's highly successful children's ministry. Using examples from Promiseland and churches of all sizes around the country, this book provides step-by-step guidance and creative application exercises to help churches develop a thriving children's ministry—one that strives to be the best hour of every kid's week. Included are Scripture-based principles and practical resources for church staff members and volunteers who agree with the critical role children's ministry plays in a local church.

Making Your Children's Ministry the Best Hour of Every Kid's Week, based on twenty-eight years of experience at Willow Creek, explains four ministry foundations: Mission, Vision, Values, and Strategy.

Content includes detailed answers to questions facing every children's ministry:

- What does Jesus expect from children's ministry?
- How can we evangelize lost kids and disciple saved kids at the same time, and should we?
- How do we engage kids so they don't become bored?
- How do we get better at recruiting and leading volunteers?
- How can our ministry be a safe place for children?
- Six specific ministry values that address the needs of today's children
- Practical first steps for ministries that want to get serious about change
- Clear indicators of success in children's ministry

Softcover: 0-310-25485-X